GEORGE MIKES

HOW TO BE A

Nicolas Bentley drew the pictures

D0180862

PENGUIN BOOKS

PENGUIN BOOKS

Published by the Penguin Group
Penguin Books Ltd, 27 Wrights Lane, London W8 5TZ, England
Penguin Putnam Inc., 375 Hudson Street, New York, New York 10014, USA
Penguin Books Australia Ltd, Ringwood, Victoria, Australia
Penguin Books Canada Ltd, 10 Alcorn Avenue, Toronto, Ontario, Canada M4V 3B2
Penguin Books (NZ) Ltd, Private Bag 102902, NSMC, Auckland, New Zealand

Penguin Books Ltd, Registered Offices: Harmondsworth, Middlesex, England

How to be an Alien first published by André Deutsch 1946
Published in Penguin Books 1966
Copyright 1946 by George Mikes and Nicolas Bentley

How to be Inimitable first published by André Deutsch 1960
Published in Penguin Books 1966
Copyright © George Mikes and Nicolas Bentley, 1960

How to be Decadent first published by André Deutsch 1977
Published in Penguin Books 1981
Copyright © George Mikes, 1977

Published in one volume as *How to be a Brit* by André Deutsch 1984
Published in Penguin Books 1986
15 17 19 20 18 16 14

Copyright © George Mikes, 1984
All rights reserved

Printed in England by Clays Ltd, St Ives plc
Typeset in Baskerville

CONTENTS

HOW TO BE INIMITABLE

I.   New English

II.   Old English

HOW TO BE DECADENT

PREFACE

Back in 1945, when André Deutsch was trying to build up a new publishing firm, he asked me if I had anything for him. I told him that I was fiddling about with some little essays which were linked by a basic idea: how to be an alien. Why I was staying on the Isle of Wight I can no longer remember, but I must have been doing so, or why would he have come there to collect the manuscript?

He enjoyed what he read, but told me that there was not enough of it for a book. So I sat down one afternoon and added five thousand more words. If anyone had said to me that I ought to take more trouble, since forty years later this book would still be selling about thirty thousand copies a year in paperback, not to mention going into a new hardback edition for which I would have to write a preface – well, I would have told that person, gently but firmly, that he or she ought to have his or her head examined. Indeed I would probably have said the same thing if told that I would still be here to write anything in forty years time, and that André would still be around – though disguised as a distinguished old boy – to publish it.

How to be an Alien was a *cri de coeur*, a desperate cry for help: oh God, look at me, I have fallen among strange people! 'But it's such a *funny* book,' people say. Perhaps it is. I hope it is. But it's not unknown for shrieks, moans, whoops and ululations to sound funny to the uninvolved.

In due course I added two further shrieks to that first one: *How to be Inimitable* in 1960, when we had started to slip but still had an Empire and refused to acknowledge much change; and *How to be Decadent* in 1977. All three books were illustrated by my great and much-missed friend, Nicolas Bentley.

During all those years since 1945, something rather curious was happening: as I strove to stop being an alien and to become a true Brit, Britain was striving to cast off its peculiar and lofty insularity and become one with the aliens, a part of the Continent (almost), just another member of the E.E.C. It oftens seems to me that I have failed in my endeavour; but compared with Britain I have succeeded gloriously.

GEORGE MIKES   *April 1984*

HOW TO BE AN
ALIEN

A HANDBOOK FOR BEGINNERS AND
ADVANCED PUPILS

'I have seen much to hate here, much to forgive. But in a world where England is finished and dead, I do not wish to live.'

ALICE DUER MILLER: *The White Cliffs*

It's easy

PREFACE TO THE 24th IMPRESSION

THE reception given to this book when it first appeared in the autumn of 1946, was at once a pleasant surprise and a disappointment for me. A surprise, because the reception was so kind; a disappointment for the same reason.

Let me explain.

The first part of this statement needs little amplification. Even people who are not closely connected with the publishing trade will be able to realize that it is very nice – I'm sorry, I'd better be a little more English: a not totally unpleasant thing for a completely unknown author to run into three impressions within a few weeks of publication and thereafter into another twenty-one.

What is my grievance, then? It is that this book has completely changed the picture I used to cherish of myself. This was to be a book of defiance. Before its publication I felt myself a man who was going to tell the English where to get off. I had spoken my mind regardless of consequences; I thought I was brave and outspoken and expected either to go unnoticed or to face a storm. But no storm came. I expected the English to be up in arms against me but they patted me on the back; I expected the British nation to rise in wrath but all they said, was: 'quite amusing'. It was indeed a bitter disappointment.

While the Rumanian Radio was serializing (without my permission) *How to be an Alien* as an anti-British tract, the Central Office of Information rang me up here in London and asked me to allow the book to be translated into Polish for the benefit of those many

Polish refugees who were then settling in this country. 'We want our friends to see us in this light,' the man said on the telephone. This was hard to bear for my militant and defiant spirit. 'But it's not such a favourable light,' I protested feebly. 'It's a very human light and that is the most favourable,' retorted the official. I was crushed.

A few weeks later my drooping spirit was revived when I heard of a suburban bank manager whose wife had brought this book home to him remarking that she had found it fairly amusing. The gentleman in question sat down in front of his open fire, put his feet up and read the book right through with a continually darkening face. When he had finished, he stood up and said:

'Downright impertinence.'

And threw the book into the fire.

He was a noble and patriotic spirit and he did me a great deal of good. I wished there had been more like him in England. But I could never find another.

Since then I have actually written about a dozen books; but I might as well have never written anything else. I remained the author of *How to be an Alien* even after I had published a collection of serious essays. Even Mr Somerset Maugham complained about this type of treatment bitterly and repeatedly. Whatever he did, he was told that he would never write another *Of Human Bondage*; Arnold Bennett in spite of fifty other works remained the author of *The Old Wives' Tale* and nothing else; and Mr Robert Graves is just the author of the Claudius books. These authors are much more eminent than I am; but their problem is the same. At the moment I am engaged in writing a 750-page picaresque novel set in ancient Sumeria. It is taking shape nicely and I am going to get the Nobel Prize for it. But it will be of no use: I shall still remain the author of *How to be an Alien*.

I am not complaining. One's books start living their independent lives soon enough, just like one's children. I love this book; it has done almost as much for me as I have done for it. Yet, however loving a parent you may be, it hurts your pride a little if you are only known, acknowledged and accepted as the father of your eldest child.

In 1946 I took this manuscript to André Deutsch, a young man who had just decided to try his luck as a publisher. He used to go, once upon a time, to the same school as my younger brother. I knew him from the old days and it was quite obvious to me even then, in Budapest, when he was only twelve and wore shorts, that he would make an excellent publisher in London if he only had the chance. So I offered my book to him and as, at that time, he could not get manuscripts from better known authors, he accepted it with a sigh. He suggested that Nicolas Bentley should be asked to 'draw the pictures'. I liked the idea but I said he would turn the suggestion down. Once again I was right: he did turn it down. Eventually, however, he was persuaded to change his mind.

Mr Deutsch was at that time working for a different firm. Four years after the publication of this book, and after the subsequent publication of three other Mikes-Bentley books, he left this firm while I stayed with them and went on working with another popular and able cartoonist, David Langdon. Now, however, André Deutsch has bought all the rights of my past and future output from his former firm and the original team of Deutsch, Bentley and myself are together again under the imprint of the first named gentleman. We are all twelve years older and Mr Deutsch does not wear shorts any more, or not in the office, at any rate.

'When are you going to write another *How to be an Alien?*' Deutsch and Bentley ask me from time to time and I am sure they mean it kindly.

They cannot quite make out the reply I mutter in answer to their friendly query. It is:

'Never, if I can help it.'

London, May 1958   GEORGE MIKES

PREFACE

I BELIEVE, without undue modesty, that I have certain qualifications to write on 'how to be an alien.' I am an alien myself. What is more, I have been an alien all my life. Only during the first twenty-six years of my life I was not aware of this plain fact. I was living in my own country, a country full of aliens, and I noticed nothing particular or irregular about myself; then I came to England, and you can imagine my painful surprise.

Like all great and important discoveries it was a matter of a few seconds. You probably all know from your schooldays how Isaac Newton discovered the law of gravitation. An apple fell on his head. This incident set him thinking for a minute or two, then he exclaimed joyfully: 'Of course! The gravitation constant is the acceleration per second that a mass of one gram causes at a distance of one centimetre.' You were also taught that James Watt one day went into the kitchen where cabbage was cooking and saw the lid of the saucepan rise and fall. 'Now let me think,' he murmured – 'let me think.' Then he struck his forehead and the steam engine was discovered. It was the same with me, although circumstances were rather different.

It was like this. Some years ago I spent a lot of time with a young lady who was very proud and conscious of being English. Once she asked me – to my great surprise – whether I would marry her. 'No,' I replied, 'I will not. My mother would never agree to my marrying a foreigner.' She looked at me a little surprised and irritated, and retorted: 'I, a foreigner? What a silly thing to say. I am English. You are the foreigner. And your mother, too.' I did not give in. 'In Budapest, too?' I asked her. 'Everywhere,' she declared with determination. 'Truth does not depend on geography. What is true in England is also true in Hungary and in North Borneo and Venezuela and everywhere.'

I saw that this theory was as irrefutable as it was simple. I was startled and upset. Mainly because of my mother whom I loved and respected. Now, I suddenly learned what she really was.

It was a shame and bad taste to be an alien, and it is no use pretending otherwise. There is no way out of it. A criminal may improve and become a decent member of society. A foreigner cannot improve. Once a foreigner, always a foreigner. There is no way out for him. He may become British; he can never become English.

So it is better to reconcile yourself to the sorrowful reality. There are some noble English people who might forgive you. There are some magnanimous souls who realize that it is not your fault, only your misfortune. They will treat you with condescension, understanding and sympathy. They will invite you to their homes. Just as they keep lap-dogs and other pets, they are quite prepared to keep a few foreigners.

The title of this book, *How to be an Alien*, consequently expresses more than it should. How to be an alien? One should not be an alien at all. There are certain rules, however, which have to be followed if you want to make yourself as acceptable and civilized as you possibly can.

Study these rules, and imitate the English. There can be only one result: if you don't succeed in imitating them you become ridiculous; if you do, you become even more ridiculous.

                                                        G. M.

I. How to be a General Alien

A WARNING TO BEGINNERS

IN ENGLAND * everything is the other way round.

On Sundays on the Continent even the poorest person puts on his best suit, tries to look respectable, and at the same time the life of the country becomes gay and cheerful; in England even the richest peer or motor-manufacturer dresses in some peculiar rags, does not shave, and the country becomes dull and dreary. On the Continent there is one topic which should be avoided – the weather; in England, if you do not repeat the phrase 'Lovely day, isn't it?' at least two hundred times a day, you are considered a bit dull. On the Continent Sunday papers appear on Monday; in England – a country of exotic oddities – they appear on Sunday. On the Continent people use a fork as though a fork were a shovel; in England they turn it upside down and push everything – including peas – on top of it.

On a continental bus approaching a request-stop the conductor rings the bell if he wants his bus to go on without stopping; in England you ring the bell if you want the bus to stop. On the Continent stray cats are judged individually on their merit – some are loved, some are only respected; in England they are universally worshipped as in ancient Egypt. On the Continent

---

* When people say England, they sometimes mean Great Britain, sometimes the United Kingdom, sometimes the British Isles – but never England.

Sabbath morn

people have good food; in England people have good table manners.

On the Continent public orators try to learn to speak fluently and smoothly; in England they take a special course in Oxonian stuttering. On the Continent learned persons love to quote Aristotle, Horace, Montaigne and show off their knowledge; in England only uneducated people show off their knowledge, nobody quotes Latin and Greek authors in the course of a conversation, unless he has never read them.

On the Continent almost every nation whether little or great has openly declared at one time or another that it is superior to all other nations; the English fight heroic wars to combat these dangerous ideas without ever mentioning which is *really* the most superior race in the world. Continental people are sensitive and touchy; the English take everything with an exquisite sense of humour – they are only offended if you tell them that they have no sense of humour. On the Continent the population consists of a small percentage of criminals, a small percentage of honest people and the rest are a vague transition between the two; in England you find a small percentage of criminals and the rest are honest people. On the other hand, people on the Continent either tell you the truth or lie; in England they hardly ever lie, but they would not dream of telling you the truth.

Many continentals think life is a game; the English think cricket is a game.

INTRODUCTION

THIS is a chapter on how to introduce people to one another.

The aim of introduction is to conceal a person's identity. It is very important that you should not pronounce anybody's name in a way that the other party may be able to catch it. Generally speaking, your pronunciation is a sound guarantee for that. On the other hand, if you are introduced to someone there are two important rules to follow.

1. If he stretches out his hand in order to shake yours, you must not accept it. Smile vaguely, and as soon as he gives up the hope of shaking you by the hand, you stretch out your own hand and try to catch *his* in vain. This game is repeated until the greater part of the afternoon or evening has elapsed. It is extremely likely that this will be the most amusing part of the afternoon or evening, anyway.

2. Once the introduction has been made you have to inquire after the health of your new acquaintance.

Try the thing in your own language. Introduce the persons, let us say, in French and murmur their names. Should they shake hands and ask:

'Comment allez-vous?'

'Comment allez-vous?' – it will be a capital joke, remembered till their last days.

Do not forget, however, that your new friend who makes this touchingly kind inquiry after your state of health does not care in the least whether you are well and kicking or dying of delirium tremens. A dialogue like this:

HE: 'How d'you do?'

YOU: 'General state of health fairly satisfactory. Slight insomnia and a rather bad corn on left foot. Blood pressure low, digestion slow but normal.'

– well, such a dialogue would be unforgivable.

In the next phase you must not say 'Pleased to meet you.' This is one of the very few lies you must never utter because, for some unknown reason, it is considered vulgar. You must not say 'Pleased to meet you,' even if you are definitely disgusted with the man.

A few general remarks:

1. Do not click your heels, do not bow, leave off gymnastic and choreographic exercises altogether for the moment.

2. Do not call foreign lawyers, teachers, dentists, commercial travellers and estate agents 'Doctor.' Everybody knows that the little word 'doctor' only means that they are Central Europeans. This is painful enough in itself, you do not need to remind people of it all the time.

Which hand will you have?

THE WEATHER

THIS is the most important topic in the land. Do not be misled by memories of your youth when, on the Continent, wanting to describe someone as exceptionally dull, you remarked: 'He is the type who would discuss the weather with you.' In England this is an ever-interesting, even thrilling topic, and you must be good at discussing the weather.

EXAMPLES FOR CONVERSATION
For Good Weather

'Lovely day, isn't it?'
'Isn't it *beautiful*?'
'The sun . . .'
'Isn't it gorgeous?'
'Wonderful, isn't it?'
'It's so nice and hot . . .'
'Personally, I think it's so nice when it's hot– isn't it?'
'I adore it – don't you?'

For Bad Weather

'Nasty day, isn't it?'
'Isn't it dreadful?'
'The rain . . . I hate rain . . .'
'I don't like it at all. Do you?'
'Fancy such a day in July. Rain in the morning, then a bit of sunshine, and then rain, rain, rain, all day long.'
'I remember exactly the same July day in 1936.'
'Yes, I remember too.'
'Or was it in 1928?'
'Yes, it was.'

'Good afternoon!'

'Or in 1939?'

'Yes, that's right.'

Now observe the last few sentences of this conversation. A very important rule emerges from it. You must never contradict anybody when discussing the weather. Should it hail and snow, should hurricanes uproot the trees from the sides of the road, and should someone remark to you: 'Nice day, isn't it?' — answer without hesitation: 'Isn't it lovely?'

Learn the above conversation by heart. If you are a bit slow in picking things up, learn at least one conversation, it would do wonderfully for any occasion.

If you do not say anything else for the rest of your life, just repeat this conversation, you still have a fair chance of passing as a remarkably witty man of sharp intellect, keen observation and extremely pleasant manners.

English society is a class society, strictly organized almost on corporative lines. If you doubt this, listen to the weather forecasts. There is always a different weather forecast for farmers. You often hear statements like this on the radio:

'To-morrow it will be cold, cloudy and foggy; long periods of rain will be interrupted by short periods of showers.'

And then:

'Weather forecast for farmers. It will be fair and warm, many hours of sunshine.'

You must not forget that the farmers do grand work of national importance and deserve better weather.

It happened on innumerable occasions that nice, warm weather had been forecast and rain and snow fell all day long, or *vice versa*. Some people jumped rashly to the conclusion that something must be wrong with the weather forecasts. They are mistaken and should be more careful with their allegations.

I have read an article in one of the Sunday papers and now I can tell you what the situation really is. All troubles are caused by anti-cyclones. (I don't quite know what anti-cyclones are, but this is not important; I hate cyclones and am very anti-cyclone myself.) The two naughtiest anti-cyclones are the Azores and the Polar anti-cyclones.

The British meteorologists forecast the *right* weather – as it really *should* be – and then these impertinent little anti-cyclones interfere and mess up everything.

That again proves that if the British kept to themselves and did not mix with foreign things like Polar and Azores anti-cyclones they would be much better off.

SOUL AND UNDERSTATEMENT

FOREIGNERS have souls; the English haven't.

On the Continent you find any amount of people who sigh deeply for no conspicuous reason, yearn, suffer and look in the air extremely sadly. This is soul.

The worst kind of soul is the great Slav soul. People who suffer from it are usually very deep thinkers. They may say things like this: 'Sometimes I am so merry and sometimes I am so sad. Can you explain why?' (You cannot, do not try.) Or they may say: 'I am so mysterious. . . . I sometimes wish I were somewhere else than where I am.' (Do not say: 'I wish you were.') Or 'When I am alone in a forest at night-time and jump from one tree to another, I often think that life is so strange.'

All this is very deep: and just soul, nothing else.

The English have no soul; they have the understatement instead.

If a continental youth wants to declare his love to a girl, he kneels down, tells her that she is the sweetest, the most charming and ravishing person in the world, that she has *something* in her, something peculiar and individual which only a few hundred thousand other women have and that he would be unable to live one more minute without her. Often, to give a little more emphasis to the statement, he shoots himself on the spot. This is a normal, week-day declaration of love in the more temperamental continental countries. In England the boy pats his adored one on the back and says softly: 'I don't object to you, you know.' If he is quite mad with passion, he may add: 'I rather fancy you, in fact.'

If he wants to marry a girl, he says:

'My soul is all an Aching Void' – John Wesley

'I say ... would you? ...'
If he wants to make an indecent proposal:
'I say ... what about ...'

Overstatement, too, plays a considerable part in English social life. This takes mostly the form of someone remarking: 'I say ...' and then keeping silent for three days on end.

TEA

THE trouble with tea is that originally it was quite a good drink.

So a group of the most eminent British scientists put their heads together, and made complicated biological experiments to find a way of spoiling it.

To the eternal glory of British science their labour bore fruit. They suggested that if you do not drink it clear, or with lemon or rum and sugar, but pour a few drops of cold milk into it, and no sugar at all, the desired object is achieved. Once this refreshing, aromatic, oriental beverage was successfully transformed into colourless and tasteless gargling-water, it suddenly became the national drink of Great Britain and Ireland — still retaining, indeed usurping, the high-sounding title of tea.

There are some occasions when you must not refuse a cup of tea, otherwise you are judged an exotic and barbarous bird without any hope of ever being able to take your place in civilised society.

If you are invited to an English home, at five o'clock in the morning you get a cup of tea. It is either brought in by a heartily smiling hostess or an almost malevolently silent maid. When you are disturbed in your sweetest morning sleep you must not say: 'Madame (or Mabel), I think you are a cruel, spiteful and malignant person who deserves to be shot.' On the contrary, you have to declare with your best five o'clock smile: 'Thank you so much. I do adore a cup of early morning tea, especially early in the morning.' If they leave you alone with the liquid, you may pour it down the wash-basin.

Then you have tea for breakfast; then you have tea at eleven o'clock in the morning; then after lunch;

The cup that cheers

then you have tea for tea; then after supper; and again at eleven o'clock at night.

You must not refuse any additional cups of tea under the following circumstances: if it is hot; if it is cold; if you are tired; if anybody thinks that you might be tired; if you are nervous; if you are gay; before you go out; if you are out; if you have just returned home; if you feel like it; if you do not feel like it; if you have had no tea for some time; if you have just had a cup.

You definitely must not follow my example. I sleep at five o'clock in the morning; I have coffee for breakfast; I drink innumerable cups of black coffee during the day; I have the most unorthodox and exotic teas even at tea-time.

The other day, for instance – I just mention this as a terrifying example to show you how low some people can sink – I wanted a cup of coffee and a piece of cheese for tea. It was one of those exceptionally hot days and my wife (once a good Englishwoman, now completely and hopelessly led astray by my wicked foreign influence) made some cold coffee and put it in the refrigerator, where it froze and became one solid block. On the other hand, she left the cheese on the kitchen table, where it melted. So I had a piece of coffee and a glass of cheese.

SEX

CONTINENTAL people have sex life; the English have hot-water bottles.

A WORD ON SOME PUBLISHERS

I HEARD of a distinguished, pure-minded English publisher who adapted John Steinbeck's novel, *The Grapes of Wrath*, so skilfully that it became a charming little family book on grapes and other fruits, with many illustrations.

On the other hand, a continental publisher in London had a French political book, *The Popular Front*, translated into English. It became an exciting, pornographic book, called *The Popular Behind*.

THE LANGUAGE

When I arrived in England I thought I knew English. After I'd been here an hour I realized that I did not understand one word. In the first week I picked up a tolerable working knowledge of the language and the the next seven years convinced me gradually but thoroughly that I would never know it really well, let alone perfectly. This is sad. My only consolation being that nobody speaks English perfectly.

Remember that those five hundred words an average Englishman uses are far from being the whole vocabulary of the language. You may learn another five hundred and another five thousand and yet another fifty thousand and still you may come across a further fifty thousand you have never heard of before, and nobody else either.

If you live here long enough you will find out to your greatest amazement that the adjective *nice* is not the only adjective the language possesses, in spite of the fact that in the first three years you do not need to learn or use any other adjectives. You can say that the weather is nice, a restaurant is nice, Mr Soandso is nice, Mrs Soandso's clothes are nice, you had a nice time, and all this will be very nice.

Then you have to decide on your accent. You will have your foreign accent all right, but many people like to mix it with something else. I knew a Polish Jew who had a strong Yiddish-Irish accent. People found it fascinating though slightly exaggerated. The easiest way to give the impression of having a good accent or no foreign accent at all is to hold an unlit pipe in your mouth, to mutter between your teeth and finish all your sentences with the question: 'isn't it?' People will not understand much, but they are accustomed to that and they will get a most excellent impression.

I have known quite a number of foreigners who tried hard to acquire an Oxford accent. The advantage of this is that you give the idea of being permanently in the company of Oxford dons and lecturers on medieval numismatics; the disadvantage is that the permanent singing is rather a strain on your throat and that it is a type of affection that even many English people find it hard to keep up incessantly. You may fall out of it, speak naturally, and then where are you?

The Mayfair accent can be highly recommended, too. The advantages of Mayfair English are that it unites the affected air of the Oxford accent with the uncultured flavour of a half-educated professional hotel-dancer.

The most successful attempts, however, to put on a highly cultured air have been made on the polysyllabic lines. Many foreigners who have learnt Latin and Greek in school discover with amazement and satisfaction that the English language has absorbed a huge amount of ancient Latin and Greek expressions, and they realize that (*a*) it is much easier to learn these expressions than the much simpler English words; (*b*) that these words as a rule are interminably long and make a simply superb impression when talking to the greengrocer, the porter and the insurance agent.

Imagine, for instance, that the porter of the block of flats where you live remarks sharply that you must not put your dustbin out in front of your door before 7.30 a.m. Should you answer 'Please don't bully me,' a loud and tiresome argument may follow, and certainly the porter will be proved right, because you are sure to find a clause in your contract (small print, bottom

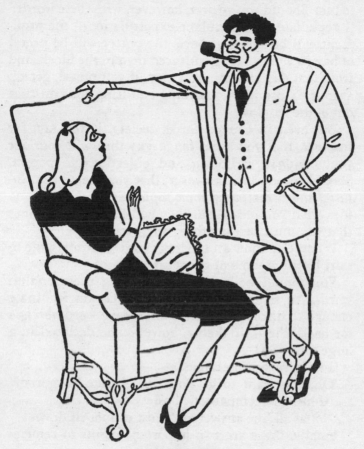

The pipe trick

of last page) that the porter is always right and you owe absolute allegiance and unconditional obedience to him. Should you answer, however, with these words: 'I repudiate your petulant expostulations,' the argument will be closed at once, the porter will be proud of having such a highly cultured man in the block, and from that day onwards you may, if you please, get up at four o'clock in the morning and hang your dustbin out of the window.

But even in Curzon Street society, if you say, for instance, that you are a *tough guy* they will consider you a vulgar, irritating and objectionable person. Should you declare, however, that you are *an inquisitorial and peremptory homo sapiens,* they will have no idea what you mean, but they will feel in their bones that you must be something wonderful.

When you know all the long words it is advisable to start learning some of the short ones, too.

You should be careful when using these endless words. An acquaintance of mine once was fortunate enough to discover the most impressive word *notalgia* for back-ache. Mistakenly, however, he declared in a large company:

'I have such a nostalgia.'

'Oh, you want to go home to Nizhne-Novgorod?' asked his most sympathetic hostess.

'Not at all.' he answered. 'I just cannot sit down.'

Finally, there are two important points to remember:

1. Do not forget that it is much easier to write in English than to speak English, because you can *write* without a foreign accent.

2. In a bus and in other public places it is more advisable to speak softly in good German than to shout in abominable English.

Anyway, this whole language business is not at all easy. After spending eight years in this country, the other day I was told by a very kind lady: 'But why do you complain? You really speak a most excellent accent without the slightest English.'

HOW NOT TO BE CLEVER

'You foreigners are so clever,' said a lady to me some years ago. First, thinking of the great amount of foreign idiots and half-wits I had had the honour of meeting, I considered this remark exaggerated but complimentary.

Since then I have learnt that it was far from it. These few words expressed the lady's contempt and slight disgust for foreigners.

If you look up the word *clever* in any English dictionary, you will find that the dictionaries are out of date and mislead you on this point. According to the Pocket Oxford Dictionary, for instance, the word means quick and neat in movement . . . skilful, talented, ingenious. Nuttall's Dictionary gives these meanings: dexterous, skilful, ingenious, quick or ready-witted, intelligent. All nice adjectives, expressing valuable and estimable characteristics. A modern Englishman, however, uses the word *clever* in the sense: shrewd, sly, furtive, surreptitious, treacherous, sneaking, crafty, un-English, un-Scottish, un-Welsh.

In England it is bad manners to be clever, to assert something confidently. It may be your own personal view that two and two make four, but you must not state it in a self-assured way, because this is a democratic country and others may be of a different opinion.

A continental gentleman seeing a nice panorama may remark:

'This view rather reminds me of Utrecht, where the peace treaty concluding the War of Spanish Succession was signed on the 11th April, 1713. The river there, however, recalls the Guadalquivir, which rises in the

'*Dr Hoffmeyer is absolutely* brilliant'

Sierra de Cazorla and flows south-west to the Atlantic Ocean and is 650 kilometres long. Oh, rivers. . . . What did Pascal say about them? "Les rivières sont les chemins qui marchent. . . ." '

This pompous, showing-off way of speaking is not permissible in England. The Englishman is modest and simple. He uses but few words and expresses so much – but so much – with them. An Englishman looking at the same view would remain silent for two or three hours and think about how to put his profound feeling into words. Then he would remark:

'It's pretty, isn't it?'

An English professor of mathematics would say to his maid checking up the shopping list:

'I'm no good at arithmetic, I'm afraid. Please correct me, Jane, if I am wrong, but I believe that the square root of 97344 is 312.'

And about knowledge. An English girl, of course, would be able to learn just a little more about, let us say, geography. But it is just not 'chic' to know whether Budapest is the capital of Roumania, Hungary or Bulgaria. And if she happens to know that Budapest *is* the capital of Roumania, she should at least be perplexed if Bucharest is mentioned suddenly.

It is so much nicer to ask, when someone speaks of Barbados, Banska Bystrica or Fiji:

'Oh those little islands. . . . Are they British?'

(They usually are.)

HOW TO BE RUDE

IT IS easy to be rude on the Continent. You just shout and call people names of a zoological character.

On a slightly higher level you may invent a few stories against your opponents. In Budapest, for instance, when a rather unpleasant-looking actress joined a nudist club, her younger and prettier colleagues spread the story that she had been accepted only under the condition that she should wear a fig-leaf on her face. Or in the same city there was a painter of limited abilities who was a most successful card-player. A colleague of his remarked once: 'What a spendthrift! All the money he makes on industrious gambling at night, he spends on his painting during the day.'

In England rudeness has quite a different technique. If somebody tells you an obviously untrue story, on the Continent you would remark 'You are a liar, Sir, and a rather dirty one at that.' In England you just say 'Oh, is that so?' Or 'That's rather an unusual story, isn't it?'

When some years ago, knowing ten words of English and using them all wrong, I applied for a translator's job, my would-be employer (or would-be-not-employer) softly remarked: 'I am afraid your English is somewhat unorthodox.' This translated into any continental language would mean: EMPLOYER (to the commissionaire): 'Jean, kick this gentleman down the steps!'

In the last century, when a wicked and unworthy subject annoyed the Sultan of Turkey or the Czar of Russia, he had his head cut of without much ceremony; but when the same happened in England, the monarch declared: 'We are not amused'; and the whole British nation even now, a century later, is immensely proud of how rude their Queen was.

Terribly rude expressions (if pronounced grimly) are: 'I am afraid that ...' 'unless ...' 'nevertheless ...' 'How queer ...' and 'I am sorry, but ...'

It is true that quite often you can hear remarks like: 'You'd better see that you get out of here!' Or 'Shut your big mouth!' Or 'Dirty pig!' etc. These remarks are very un-English and are the results of foreign influence. (Dating back, however, to the era of the Danish invasion.)

'Chameau!'

HOW TO COMPROMISE

WISE compromise is one of the basic principles and virtues of the British.

If a continental greengrocer asks 14 schillings (or crowns, or francs, or pengoes, or dinars or leis or δραχμαί or лева, or whatever you like) for a bunch of radishes, and his customer offers 2, and finally they strike a bargain agreeing on 6 schillings, francs, roubles, etc., this is just the low continental habit of bargaining; on the other hand, if the British dock-workers or any workers claim a rise of 4 shillings per day, and the employers first flatly refuse even a penny, but after six weeks strike they agree to a rise of 2 shillings per day – that is yet another proof of the British genius for compromise. Bargaining is a repulsive habit; compromise is one of the highest human virtues – the difference between the two being that the first is practised on the Continent, the latter in Great Britain.

The genius for compromise has another aspect, too. It has a tendency to unite together everything which is bad. English club life, for instance, unites the liabilities of social life with the boredom of solitude. An average English house combines all the curses of civilisation with the vicissitudes of life in the open. It is all right to have windows, but you must not have double windows because double windows would indeed stop the wind from blowing right into the room, and after all, you must be fair and give the wind a chance. It is all right to have central heating in an English home, except the bath room, because that is the only place where you are naked *and* wet at the same time, and you must give British germs a fair chance. The open

A Balkan bargain

fire is an accepted, indeed a traditional, institution. You sit in front of it and your face is hot whilst your back is cold. It is a fair compromise between two extremes and settles the problem of how to burn and catch cold at the same time. The fact that you may have a drink at five past six p.m., but that it is a criminal offence to have it at five to six is an extremely wise compromise between two things (I do not quite know between what, certainly not between prohibition and licentiousness), achieving the great aim that nobody can get drunk between three o'clock and six o'clock in the afternoon unless he wants to and drinks at home.

English spelling is a compromise between documentary expressions and an elaborate code-system; spending three hours in a queue in front of a cinema is a compromise between entertainment and asceticism; the English weather is a fair compromise between rain and fog; to employ an English charwoman is a compromise between having a dirty house or cleaning it yourself; Yorkshire pudding is a compromise between a pudding and the county of Yorkshire.

The Labour Party is a fair compromise between Socialism and Bureaucracy; the Beveridge Plan is a fair compromise between being and not being a Socialist at the same time; the Liberal Party is a fair compromise between the Beveridge Plan and Toryism; the Independent Labour Party is a fair compromise between Independent Labour and a political party; the Tory-reformers are a fair compromise between revolutionary conservatism and retrograde progress; and the whole British political life is a huge and non-compromising fight between compromising Conservatives and compromising Socialists.

HOW TO BE A HYPOCRITE

IF YOU want to be really and truly British, you must become a hypocrite.

Now: how to be a hypocrite?

As some people say that an example explains things better than the best theory, let me try this way.

I had a drink with an English friend of mine in a pub. We were sitting on the high chairs in front of the counter when a flying bomb exploded about a hundred yards away. I was truly and honestly frightened, and when a few seconds later I looked around, I could not see my friend anywhere. At last I noticed that he was lying on the floor, flat as a pancake. When he realized that nothing particular had happened in the pub he got up a little embarrassed, flicked the dust off his suit, and turned to me with a superior and sarcastic smile.

'Good Heavens! Were you so frightened that you couldn't move?'

ABOUT SIMPLE JOYS

IT IS important that you should learn to enjoy simple joys, because that is extremely English. All serious Englishmen play darts and cricket and many other games; a famous English statesman was reported to be catching butterflies in the interval between giving up two European states to the Germans; there was even some misunderstanding with the French because they considered the habit of English soldiers of singing and playing football and hide and seek and blind man's buff slightly childish.

Dull and pompous foreigners are unable to understand why ex-cabinet ministers get together and sing 'Daisy, Daisy' in choir; why serious business men play with toy locomotives while their children learn trigonometry in the adjoining room; why High Court judges collect rare birds when rare birds are rare and they cannot collect many in any case; why it is the ambition of grown-up persons to push a little ball into a small hole; why a great politician who saved England and made history is called a 'jolly good fellow.'

They cannot grasp why people sing when alone and yet sit silent and dumb for hours on end in their clubs, not uttering a word for months in the most distinguished company, and pay twenty guineas a year for the privilege.

Birds of a feather

THE NATIONAL PASSION

QUEUEING is the national passion of an otherwise dispassionate race. The English are rather shy about it, and deny that they adore it.

On the Continent, if people are waiting at a bus-stop they loiter around in a seemingly vague fashion. When the bus arrives they make a dash for it; most of them leave by the bus and a lucky minority is taken away by an elegant black ambulance car. An Englishman, even if he is alone, forms an orderly queue of one.

The biggest and most attractive advertisements in front of cinemas tell people: Queue here for 4s 6d; Queue here for 9s 3d; Queue here for 16s 8d (inclusive of tax). Those cinemas which do not put out these queueing signs do not do good business at all.

At week-ends an Englishman queues up at the bus-stop, travels out to Richmond, queues up for a boat, then queues up for tea, then queues up for ice cream, then joins a few more odd queues just for the sake of the fun of it, then queues up at the bus-stop and has the time of his life.

Many English families spend lovely evenings at home just by queueing up for a few hours, and the parents are very sad when the children leave them and queue up for going to bed.

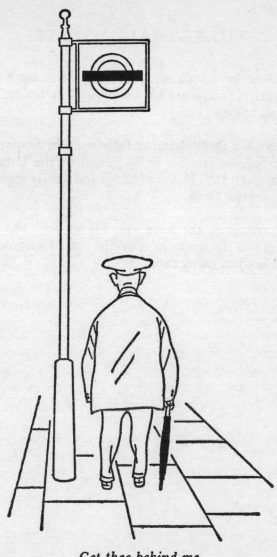

Get thee behind me

THREE SMALL POINTS

IF YOU go for a walk with a friend, don't say a word for hours; if you go out for a walk with your dog, keep chatting to him.

There is a three-chamber legislation in England. A bill to become law has to be passed by the House of Commons and the House of Lords and finally approved by the Brains Trust.

A fishmonger is the man who mongs fish; the iron-monger and the warmonger do the same with iron and war. They just mong them.

*And will you be going to Cruft's this year as usual,
Florence?*

II. How to be a Particular Alien

A BLOOMSBURY INTELLECTUAL

THEY all hate uniforms so much that they all wear a special uniform of their own: brown velvet trousers, canary yellow pullover, green jacket with sky-blue checks.

The suit of clothes has to be chosen with the utmost care and is intended to prove that its wearer does not care for suits and other petty, worldly things.

A walking-stick, too, is often carried by the slightly dandyfied right-wing of the clan.

A golden chain around the ankle, purple velvet shoes and a half-wild angora cat on the shoulders are strongly recommended as they much increase the appearance of arresting casualness.

It is extremely important that the B.I. should *always* wear a three-days beard, as shaving is considered a contemptible bourgeois habit. (The extremist left-wing holds the same view concerning washing, too.) First one will find it a little trying to shave one's four-day beard in such a way that, after shaving, a three days old beard ration should be left on the cheeks, but practise and devoted care will bring their fruits.

A certain amount of rudeness is quite indispensable, because you have to prove day and night that the silly little commonplace rules and customs of society are not meant for *you*. If you find it too difficult to give up these little habits – to say 'Hullo' and 'How d'you do?' and 'Thank you,' etc. – because owing to Auntie

Ars longa, vita brevis

Betty's or Tante Bertha's strict upbringing they have become second nature, then join a Bloomsbury school for bad manners, and after a fortnight you will feel no pang of conscience when stepping deliberately on the corn of the venerable literary editor of a quarterly magazine in the bus.

Literary opinions must be most carefully selected. Statements like this are most impressive. 'There have been altogether two real poets in England: Sir Thomas Wyatt and John Ford. The works of the rest are rubbish.' Of course, you should include, as the third really great, colossal and epoch-making talent your own friend, T. B. Williams, whose neo-expressionist poetry is so terribly deep that the overwhelming majority of editors do not understand it and refuse to publish it. T. B. Williams, you may proudly claim, has never used a comma or a full stop, and what is more, he has improved Apollinaire's and Aragon's primitive technique by the fact that he *does* use question marks. (The generous and extravagant praise of T. B. Williams is absolutely essential, otherwise who will praise *you*?)

As to your own literary activities, your poems, dramas and great novels may lie at the bottom of your drawer in manuscript form. But it is important that you should publish a few literary reviews, scolding and disparaging everything and everybody on earth from a very superior and high-brow point of view, quoting Sir Thomas Wyatt and anything in French and letting the reader feel what *you* would be able to do if you could only find a publisher.

(Some practical advice. It is not difficult to have a few literary reviews published. Many weeklies and monthlies would publish anything in their so-called literary columns, if it costs nothing. You must not call your action unfair competition with qualified

T. B. Williams

reviewers; call it devotion to the 'cause.' Almost every paper has a cause – if yours has not, invent one, it is quite easy. And it really does not matter what you write. I remember one B.I. writing of a significant philosophical work and admitting in the opening sentence that he did not understand it; still, I suppose the review passed as buoyant and alarmingly sincere.)

Politically you must belong to the extreme left. You must, however, bear a few things in mind:

1. You must not care a damn about the welfare of the people in this country or abroad, because that would be 'practical politics' – and you should only be interested in the ideological side of matters.

2. Do not belong to any party, because that would be 'regimentation.' Whatever different parties achieve, it is much more interesting to criticize everyone than to belong to the herd.

3. Do not hesitate to scorn Soviet Russia as reactionary and imperialistic, the British Labour Party as a conglomeration of elderly Trade Union Blimps, the French Socialists as 'confused people,' the other Western Socialist parties as meek, bourgeois clubs, the American labour movements as being in the pay of big business; and call all republicans, communists, anarchists and nihilists 'backward, reactionary crypto-fascists.'

You should also invent a few truly original, constructive theories too, such as:

Only Brahmanism can save the world.

Spiritualism is a factor, growing immensely in importance, and a practical, working coalition between ghosts and Trotskyites would be highly desirable.

The abolition of all taxation would enrich the population so enormously that everybody would be able to pay much more taxes than before.

Finally, remember the main point. *Always* be original! It is not as difficult as it sounds: you just have to copy the habits and sayings of a few thousand other B.I.s.

MAYFAIR PLAYBOY

FIX THE little word *de* in front of your name. It has a remarkable attraction. I knew a certain Leo Rosenberg from Graz who called himself Lionel de Rosenberg and was a huge success in Deanery Mews as a Tyrolean nobleman.

Believe that the aim of life is to have a nice time, go to nice places and meet nice people. (Now: to have a nice time means to have two more drinks daily than you can carry; nice places are the halls of great hotels, intimate little clubs, night clubs and private houses with large radiograms and no bookshelves; nice people are those who say silly things in good English – nasty people are those who drop clever remarks as well as their aitches.)

In the old days the man who had no money was not considered a gentleman. In the era of an enlightened Mayfair this attitude has changed. A gentleman may have money or may sponge on his friends; the criterion of a gentleman is that however poor he may be he still refuse to do useful work.

You have to develop your charm with the greatest care. Always laugh at everybody's jokes – but be careful to tell a joke from a serious and profound observation. Be polite in a teasing, nonchalant manner. Sneer at everything you are not intelligent enough to understand. You may flirt with anybody's wife, but respect the ties of illegitimate friendships – unless you have a really good opportunity which it would be such a pity to miss. Don't forget that well-pressed trousers, carefully knotted ties and silk shirts are the greatest of all human values. Never be sober after 6.30 p.m.

Nice versus *nasty*

HOW TO BE A FILM PRODUCER

A LITTLE foreign blood is very advantageous, almost essential, to become a really great British film producer.

The first aim of a British film producer should be to teach Hollywood a lesson. Do not be misled, however, by the examples of *Henry V* or *Pygmalion*, which tend to prove that excellent films can be made of great plays without changing the out-of-date words of Shakespeare and the un-film-like dialogues of Shaw by ten 'experts' who really know better.

Forget these misleading examples because it is obvious that Shakespeare could not possibly have had any film technique, and recent research has proved that he did not even have an eight-seater saloon car with his own uniformed chauffeur.

You must not touch any typically American subject. For instance: a young man of Carthage (Kentucky) who can whistle beautifully goes to town, and after many disappointments forms his own swing-band and becomes the leading conductor of New York's night life – which, if you can take the implication of Hollywood films seriously, is one of the highest honours which can be conferred on anyone in that country. At the same time he falls in love with the cloakroom attendant of a drug-store* round the corner, a platinum-blonde, ravishingly beautiful, who sings a little better than Galli Curci and Deanna Durbin rolled into one and, in secret, has the greatest histrionic talent

* Please note my extensive knowledge of the American language.

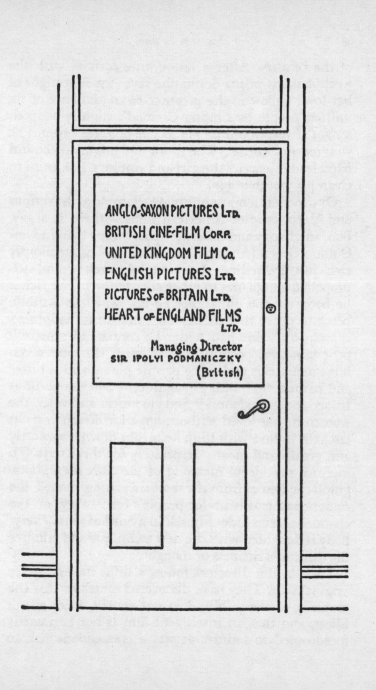

of the century. After a last-minute scandal with the world-famous prima donna she saves the first night of her lover's show in the presence of an audience of six million people by singing Gounod's slightly adapted song. ('If you would be *my* tootsie-bootsie, I would be *your* tootsie-bootsie'.) The young and mighty successful band-leader marries the girl and employs Toscanini to clean his mouth-organ.

Or – to mention just one more example of the serious and 'deep' type of American films – there is a gay, buoyant, happy and miserably poor young man in New Golders Green (Alabama), who becomes tremendously rich just by selling thousands of tractors and jet-propelled aeroplanes to other poor fellows. The richer he becomes, the unhappier he is – which is a subtle point to prove that money does not mean happiness, consequently one had better be content to remain a poor labourer, possibly unemployed. He buys seven huge motor cars and three private planes and is bitter and pained; he builds a magnificent and ostentatious palace and gets gloomier and gloomier; and when the woman he has loved without hope for fifteen years at last falls in love with him, he breaks down completely and groans and moans desperately for three days. To increase the 'deep' meaning of the film they photograph the heroes from the most surprising angles: the cameraman crawls under people's feet, swings on the chandelier, and hides himself in a bowl of soup. Everybody is delighted with the new technique and admires the director's richness of thought.

English film directors follow a different and quite original line. They have discovered somehow that the majority of the public does not consist, after all, of idiots, and that an intelligent film is not necessarily foredoomed to failure. It was a tremendous risk to

'I understand they then knocked them in the Old Kent Road'

make experiments based on this assumption, but it
has proved worth while.

There are certain rules you must bear in mind if
you want to make a really and truly British film.

1. The 'cockney heart' has definitely been discovered, *i.e.* the fact that even people who drop their
aitches have a heart. The discovery was originally made
by Mr Noel Coward, who is reported to have met a
man who knew someone who had actually seen a cockney from quite near. Ever since it has been essential
that a cockney should figure in every British film and
display his heart throughout the performance.

2. It has also been discovered that ordinary men
occasionally use unparliamentary expressions in the
course of their every-day conversation. It has been
decided that the more often the adjective referring to
the sanguinary character of certain things or persons is
used and the exclamation 'Damn!' is uttered, the more
realistic and more convincing the film becomes, as able
seamen and flight-sergeants sometimes go so far as to
say 'Damn!' when they are carried away by passion. All
bodies and associations formed to preserve the purity
of the English soul should note that I do not agree
with this habit – I simply record it. But as it is a habit,
the author readily agrees to supply by correspondence
a further list of the most expressive military terms
which would make any new film surprisingly realistic.

3. Nothing should be good enough for a British film
producer. I have heard of a gentleman (I don't know
whether the story is true, or only characteristic) who
made a film about Egypt and had a sphinx built in the
studio. When he and his company sailed to Egypt to
make some exterior shots, he took his own sphinx with
him to the desert. He was quite right, because first of

all the original sphinx is very old and film people should not use second-hand stuff; secondly, the old sphinx might have been good enough for Egyptians (who are all foreigners, after all) but not for a British film company.

4. As I have seen political events successfully filmed as detective-stories, and historical personages appear as 'great lovers' (and nothing else), I have come to the conclusion that this slight change in the character of a person is highly recommendable, and I advise the filming of *Peter Pan* as a thriller, and the *Concise Oxford Dictionary* as a comic opera.

DRIVING CARS

IT IS about the same to drive a car in England as anywhere else. To change a punctured tyre in the wind
and rain gives about the same pleasure outside London
as outside Rio de Janeiro; it is not more fun to try to
start up a cold motor with the handle in Moscow than
in Manchester, the roughly 50–50 proportion between
driving an average car and *pushing* it is the same in
Sydney and Edinburgh.

There are, however, a few characteristics which distinguish the English motorist from the continental,
and some points which the English motorist has to
remember.

1. In English towns there is a thirty miles an hour
speed-limit and the police keep a watchful eye on
law-breakers. The fight against reckless driving is
directed extremely skilfully and carefully according
to the very best English detective-traditions. It is practically impossible to find out whether you are being
followed by a police car or not. There are, however, a
few indications which may help people of extraordi-
nary intelligence and with very keen powers of
observation:

(a) The police always use a 13 h.p., blue Wolseley
car;

(*b*) three uniformed policemen sit in it; and

(*c*) on these cars you can read the word POLICE
written in large letters in front and rear, all in capitals
– lit up during the hours of darkness.

2. I think England is the only country in the world
where you have to leave your lights on even if you park

Say not the struggle naught availeth – A. H. Clough

in a brilliantly lit-up street. The advantage being that your battery gets exhausted, you cannot start up again and consequently the number of road accidents are greatly reduced. Safety first!

3. Only motorists can answer this puzzling question: What are taxis for? A simple pedestrian knows that they are certainly not there to carry passengers.

Taxis, in fact, are a Christian institution. They are here to teach drivers modesty and humility. They teach us never to be over-confident; they remind us that we never can tell what the next moment will bring for us, whether we shall be able to drive on or a taxi will bump into us from the back or the side. '. . . and thou shalt fear day and night, and shalt have none assurance of thy life' (Deut., chapter 28, verse 66).

4. There is a huge ideological warfare going on behind the scenes of the motorist world.

Whenever you stop your car in the City, the West End or many other places, two or three policemen rush at you and tell you that you must not park *there*. Where may you park? They shrug their shoulders. There are a couple of spots on the South Coast and in a village called Minchinhampton. Three cars may park there for half an hour every other Sunday morning between 7 and 8 a.m.

The police are perfectly right. After all, cars have been built to run, and run fast, so they should not stop.

This healthy philosophy of the police has been seriously challenged by a certain group of motorists who maintain that cars have been built to park and not to move. These people drive out to Hampstead Heath or Richmond on beautiful, sunny days, pull up all their windows and go to sleep. They do not get a spot of air; they are miserably uncomfortable; they have nightmares, and the whole procedure is called 'spending a lovely afternoon in the open.'

THREE GAMES FOR BUS DRIVERS

IF YOU become a bus driver there are three lovely and very popular games you must learn to play.

1. *Blind man's buff.* When you turn right just signal by showing two millimetres of your finger-tips. It is great fun when motorists do not notice your signal and run into your huge bus with their tiny cars.

2. *Hide and seek.* Whenever you approach a request stop hide behind a large lorry or another bus and when you have almost reached the stop shoot off at a terrific speed. It is very amusing to see people shake their fists at you. It is ten to one they miss some important business appointment.

3. *Hospital game.* If you have to stop for one reason or another, never wait until the conductor rings the bell. If you start moving quickly and unexpectedly, and if you are lucky – and in slippery weather you have a very good chance – people will fall on top of one another. This looks extremely funny from the driver's seat. (Sometimes the people themselves, who fall into a muddy pool and break their legs, make a fuss, but, alas! every society has its bores who have no sense of humour and cannot enjoy a joke at their own expense.)

You can't catch me!

HOW TO PLAN A TOWN

BRITAIN, far from being a 'decadent democracy', is a Spartan country. This is mainly due to the British way of building towns, which dispenses with the reasonable comfort enjoyed by all the other weak and effeminate peoples of the world.

Medieval warriors wore steel breast-plates and leggings not only for defence but also to keep up their fighting spirit; priests of the Middle Ages tortured their bodies with hair-shirts; Indian yogis take their daily nap lying on a carpet of nails to remain fit. The English plan their towns in such a way that these replace the discomfort of steel breast-plates, hair-shirts and nail-carpets.

On the Continent doctors, lawyers, booksellers – just to mention a few examples – are sprinkled all over the city, so you can call on a good or at least expensive doctor in any district. In England the idea is that it is the address that makes the man. Doctors in London are crowded in Harley Street, solicitors in Lincoln's Inn Fields, second-hand-bookshops in Charing Cross Road, newspaper offices in Fleet Street, tailors in Saville Row, car-merchants in Great Portland Street, theatres around Piccadilly Circus, cinemas in Leicester Square, etc. If you have a chance of replanning London you can greatly improve on this idea. All greengrocers should be placed in Hornsey Lane (N6), all butchers in Mile End (E1), and all gentlemen's conveniences in Bloomsbury (WC).

Now I should like to give you a little practical advice on how to build an English town.

Mortification of the flesh

You must understand that an English town is a vast conspiracy to mislead foreigners. You have to use century-old little practices and tricks.

1. First of all, never build a street straight. The English love privacy and do not want to see one end of the street from the other end. Make sudden curves in the streets and build them S-shaped too; the letters L, T, V, Y, W and O are also becoming increasingly popular. It would be a fine tribute to the Greeks to build a few Φ and Θ-shaped streets; it would be an ingenious compliment to the Russians to favour the shape Я, and I am sure the Chinese would be more than flattered to see some 幽-shaped thoroughfares.

2. Never build the houses of the same street in a straight line. The British have always been a freedom-loving race and the 'freedom to build a muddle' is one of their most ancient civic rights.

3. Now there are further camouflage possibilities in the numbering of houses. Primitive continental races put even numbers on one side, odd numbers on the other, and you always know that small numbers start from the north or west. In England you have this system, too; but you may start numbering your houses at one end, go up to a certain number on the same side, then continue on the other side, going back in the opposite direction.

You may leave out some numbers if you are superstitious; and you may continue the numbering in a side street; you may also give the same number to two or three houses.

But this is far from the end. Many people refuse to have numbers altogether, and they choose names. It is very pleasant, for instance, to find a street with three hundred and fifty totally similar bungalows and look for 'The Bungalow'. Or to arrive in a street where all the houses have a charming view of a hill and try to find 'Hill View'. Or search for 'Seven Oaks' and find a house with three apple-trees.

4. Give a different name to the street whenever it bends; but if the curve is so sharp that it really makes two different streets, you may keep the same name. On the other hand, if, owing to neglect, a street has been built in a straight line it must be called by many different names (High Holborn, New Oxford Street, Oxford Street, Bayswater Road, Notting Hill Gate, Holland Park and so on).

5. As some cute foreigners would be able to learn their way about even under such circumstances, some further precautions are necessary. Call streets by various names: street, road, place, mews, crescent, avenue, rise, lane, way, grove, park, gardens, alley, arch, path, walk, broadway, promenade, gate, terrace, vale, view, hill, etc.*

Now two further possibilities arise:

(*a*) Gather all sorts of streets and squares of the same name in one neighbourhood: Belsize Park, Belsize

---

* While this book was at the printers a correspondence in *The Times* showed that the English have almost sixty synonyms for 'street.' If you add to these the street names which stand alone (Piccadilly, Strand, etc.) and the accepted and frequently used double names ('Garden Terrace', 'Church Street', 'Park Road', etc.) the number of street names reaches or exceeds a hundred. It has been suggested by one correspondent that this clearly proves what wonderful imagination the English have. I believe it proves the contrary. A West End street in London is not called 'Haymarket' because the playful fancy of Londoners populates the district with romantically clad medieval food dealers, but simply because they have not noticed as yet that the hay trade has considerably declined between Piccadilly and Pall Mall in the last three hundred years.

Street, Belsize Road, Belsize Gardens, Belsize Green, Belsize Circus, Belsize Yard, Belsize Viaduct, Belsize Arcade, Belsize Heath, etc.

(*b*) Place a number of streets of *exactly* the same name in different districts. If you have about twenty Princes Squares and Warwick Avenues in the town, the muddle – you may claim without immodesty – will be complete.

6. Street names should be painted clearly and distinctly on large boards. Then hide these boards carefully. Place them too high or too low, in shadow and darkness, upside down and inside out, or, even better, lock them up in a safe in your bank, otherwise they may give people some indication about the names of the streets.

7. In order to break down the foreigner's last vestige of resistance and shatter his morale, one further trick is advisable: Introduce the system of squares – real squares, I mean – which run into four streets like this:

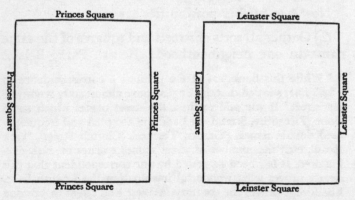

With this simple device it is possible to build a street of which the two sides have different names.

P.S. – I have been told that my above-described theory

is all wrong and is only due to my Central European conceit, because the English do not care for the opinion of foreigners. In every other country, it has been explained, people just build streets and towns following their own common scnsc. England is the only country of the world where there is a Ministry of Town and Country Planning. That is the real reason for the muddle.

CIVIL SERVANT

THERE is a world of difference between the English Civil Servant and the continental.

On the Continent (not speaking now of the Scandinavian countries), Civil Servants assume a certain military air. They consider themselves little generals; they use delaying tactics; they cannot withdraw armies, so they withdraw permissions; they thunder like cannons and their speech is like machine-gun fire; they cannot lose battles, they lose documents instead. They consider that the sole aim of human society is to give jobs to Civil Servants. A few wicked individuals, however (contemptible little groups of people who are not Civil Servants), conspire against them, come to them with various requests, complaints, problems, etc., with the sole purpose of making a nuisance of themselves. These people get the reception they deserve. They are kept waiting in cold and dirty ante-chambers (some of them clean these rooms occasionally, but they are hired commissionaires whose duty it is to re-dirty these rooms every morning); they have to stand, often at attention, whilst they are spoken to; they are always shouted at in a rude manner and their requests are turned down with malicious pleasure. Sometimes – this is a popular cat and mouse game – they are sent to another office on the fifth floor, from there they are directed to a third office in the basement, where they are told that they should not have come there at all and sent back to the original office. In that office they are thoroughly told off in acrimonious language and dispatched to the fifth floor once again, from there to the basement and the procedure goes on endlessly until the poor fellows

'*Alors, ECOUTEZ madame –*'

either get tired of the whole business and give up in despair or become raving lunatics and go to an asylum asking for admittance. If the latter case occurs they are told in the reception office that they have come to the wrong place, they should go to another office on the fifth floor, from which they are sent down to the basement, etc., etc., until they give up being lunatics.

(If you want to catch me out and ask me who are then the people who fill the continental lunatic asylums, I can give you the explanation: they are all Civil Servants who know the ways and means of dealing with officials and succeed in getting in somehow.)

If a former continental Civil Servant thought that this martial behaviour would be accepted by the British public he would be badly mistaken. The English Civil Servant considers himself no soldier but a glorified businessman. He is smooth and courteous; he smiles in a superior way; he is agreeable and obliging.

If so – you may ask – how can he achieve the supreme object of his vast and noble organization, namely, not to transact any business and be left in peace to read a good murder story undisturbed?

There are various, centuries-old, true British traditions to secure this aim.

1. All orders and directives to the public are worded in such a way that they should have no meaning whatever.

2. All official letters are written in such a language that the oracles of Delphi sound as examples of clear, outspoken, straightforward statements compared with them.

3. Civil Servants never make decisions, they only promise to 'consider,' – 'consider favourably' – or – and this is the utmost – 'reconsider' certain questions.

4. In principle the British Civil Servant stands always at the disposal of the public. In practice he is either in 'conference' or out for lunch, or in but having his tea, or just out. Some develop an admirable technique of going out for tea before coming back from lunch.

The British Civil Servant, unlike the rough bully we often find on the Continent, is the Obedient Servant of the public. Before the war, an alien in this country was ordered to leave. He asked for extension of his staying permit, but was refused. He stayed on all the same, and after a while he received the following letter (I quote from memory):

Dear Sir,
    The Under-Secretary of State presents his compliments and regrets that he is unable to reconsider your case, and begs to inform you that unless you kindly leave this country within 24 hours you will be forcibly expelled.

Your Obedient Servant,
x x x

On the Continent rich and influential people, or those who have friends, cousins, brothers-in-law, tenants, business associates, etc., in an office may have their requests fulfilled. In England there is no such corruption and your obedient servant just will not do a thing whoever you may be. And this is the real beauty of democracy.

JOURNALISM OR THE FREEDOM OF THE PRESS

The Fact

THERE was some trouble with the Buburuk tribe in the Pacific Island, Charamak. A party of ten English and two American soldiers, under the command of Capt. R. L. A. T. W. Tilbury, raided the island and took 217 revolutionary, native troublemakers prisoner and wrecked two large oil-dumps. The party remained ashore an hour-and-a-half and returned to their base without loss to themselves.

How to report this event? It depends which newspaper you work for.

THE TIMES

... It would be exceedingly perilous to overestimate the significance of the raid, but it can be fairly proclaimed that it would be even more dangerous to underestimate it. The success of the raid clearly proves that the native defences are not invulnerable; it would be fallacious and deceptive, however, to conclude that these defences are vulnerable. The number of revolutionaries captured cannot be safely stated, but it seems likely that the number is well over 216 but well under 218.

IN THE HOUSE

You may become an M.P. (Nothing is impossible – this would not be even unprecedented.) You may hear then the following statement by a member of Her Majesty's Government:

'Concerning the two wrecked oil-dumps I can give

this information to the House. In the first half of this year the amount of native oil destroyed by the Army, Navy and the R.A.F. – excluding however, the Fleet Air Arm – is one-half as much as three times the amount destroyed during the corresponding months of the previous year, seven and a half times as much as the two-fifths destroyed two years ago and three-quarters as much again as twelve times one-sixth destroyed three years ago.' (Loud cheers from the Government benches.)

You jump to your feet and ask this question:

YOU: Is the Right Hon. Gentleman aware that people in this country are puzzled and worried by the fact that Charamak was raided and not Ragamak?

THE RIGHT HON. MEMBER: I have nothing to add to my statement given on 2nd August, 1892.

EVENING STANDARD
(Londoner's Diary)

The most interesting feature of the Charamak raid is the fact that Reggie Tilbury is the fifth son of the Earl of Bayswater. He was an Oxford Blue, a first-class cricketer and quite good at polo. When I talked to his wife (Lady Clarisse, the daughter of Lord Elasson) at Claridges today, she wore a black suit and a tiny black hat with a yellow feather in it. She said: 'Reggie was always very much interested in warfare.' Later she remarked: 'It was clever of him, wasn't it?'

You may write a letter to the Editor of *The Times*:

Sir, – In connection with the Charamak raid I should like to mention as a matter of considerable interest that it was in that little Pacific Island that the distinguished English poet, John Flat, wrote his famous poem 'The Cod' in 1693. Yours, etc. . . .

An early interest in warfare

You may read this answer on the following day.

Sir, – I am very grateful to Mr . . . for calling attention to John Flat's poem 'The Cod.' May I be allowed to use this opportunity, however, to correct a widespread and in my view very unfortunate error which the great masses of the British people seem to share with your correspondent. 'The Cod,' although John Flat started writing it in 1693, was only finished in the early days of January 1694.

Yours, etc. . . .

If you are the London correspondent of the American paper

THE OKLAHOMA SUN

simply cable this:

'Yanks Conquer Pacific Ocean.'

IF NATURALIZED

THE VERB *to naturalize* clearly proves what the British think of you. Before you are admitted to British citizenship you are not even considered a natural human being. I looked up the word natural (na'tural) in the Pocket Oxford Dictionary (p. 251); it says: *Of or according to or provided by nature, physically existing, innate, instinctive, normal, not miraculous or spiritual or artificial or conventional....* Note that before you obtain British citizenship, they simply doubt that you are provided by nature.

According to the Pocket Oxford Dictionary the word 'natural' has a second meaning, too: *Half-witted person.* This second meaning, however, is irrelevant from the point of view of our present argument.

If you are tired of not being provided by nature, not being physically existing and being miraculous and

conventional at the same time, apply for British citizenship. Roughly speaking, there are two possibilities: it will be granted to you, or not.

In the first case you must recognize and revise your attitude to life. You must pretend that you are everything you are not and you must look down upon everything you are.

Copy the attitude of an English acquaintance of mine – let us call him Gregory Baker. He, an English solicitor, feels particularly deep contempt for the following classes of people: foreigners, Americans, Frenchmen, Irishmen, Scotsmen and Welshmen, Jews, workers, clerks, poor people, non-professional men, business men, actors, journalists and literary men, women, solicitors who do not practise in his immediate neighbourhood, solicitors who are hard up and solicitors who are too rich, Socialists, Liberals, Tory-reformers (Communists are not worthy even of his contempt); he looks down upon his mother, because she has a business mind, his wife, because she comes from a non-professional county family, his brother, because although he is a professional officer he does not serve with the Guards, Hussars, or at least with a county regiment. He adores and admires his seven-years old son, because the shape of his nose resembles his own.

If naturalized, remember these rules:

1. You must start eating porridge for breakfast and allege that you like it.

2. Speak English with your former compatriots. Deny that you know any foreign language (including your mother tongue). The knowledge of foreign languages is very un-English. A little French is permissible, but only with an atrocious accent.

3. Revise your library. Get rid of all foreign writers

whether in the original or translated into English. The works of Dostoyevsky should be replaced by a volume on English Birds; the collected works of Proust by a book called 'Interior Decoration in the Regency Period'; and Pascal's *Pensées* by the 'Life and Thoughts of a Scottish Salmon'.

4. Speaking of your new compatriots, always use the first person plural.

In this aspect, though, a certain caution is advisable. I know a na'turalized Britisher who, talking to a young man, repeatedly used the phrase 'We Englishmen.' The young man looked at him, took his pipe out of his mouth and remarked softly: 'Sorry, Sir, I'm a Welshman,' turned his back on him and walked away.

The same gentleman was listening to a conversation. It was mentioned that the Japanese had claimed to have shot down 22 planes.

'What – ours?' he asked indignantly.

His English hostess answered icily:

'No – *ours*.'

HOW TO BE AN
INIMITABLE

COMING OF AGE IN ENGLAND

The sincerest form of flattery

COMING OF AGE

IT was twenty-one years ago that England and I first set foot on each other. I came for a fortnight; I have stayed ever since. As a man I am in my forties; as an inhabitant of Britain I am just twenty-one. I was only seven when my first child was born. I have come of age; which is more than England can boast of.

In these past twenty-one years England has gained me and lost an Empire. The net gain was small. I used to pronounce my name Me-cash but nowadays most people say Mikes to rhyme with *likes*. The Empire now pronounces its name *Commonwealth* – to rhyme with nothing at all.

Many things have changed in the last two decades. The Britain of 1960 is vastly different from the Britain of 1938, and even from the Britain of 1946, when I first published my impressions of this country under the title *How to be an Alien*. The time has come, I feel, to revisit England.

When I first came here, Englishmen were slim and taciturn, while today they are slim and taciturn. Then, they were grunting and inscrutable; today they are grunting and inscrutable. Then, they were honest, likeable but not too quick on the uptake; today they are honest, likeable but no quicker on the uptake. Then, they kept discussing the weather rather dully; today they keep discussing the weather much more dully. Then, their main interests were cricket, horses and dogs, while today their main interests are dogs, horses and cricket. Then, the main newspaper topics

were sex, crime and money, while today it is money,
money, money and crime with a little sex somewhat
perfunctorily thrown in. Then, Britain was being in-
undated by blooming* foreigners and she did not like
it. Today foreigners are called *visitors, tourists* and
other fancy names – and in extreme emergency, when
shortage of foreign currency is too pressing – even
Distinguished Europeans. We must all exercise the
greatest care, because the resemblance between a Distinguished European and a bloody foreigner is most
misleading.

Then, Britons travelled to the Continent, drank tea
with milk in Paris, ate roast beef and Yorkshire pudding in Monte Carlo, kept to one another's company
everywhere and were proud of their insularity; today
they drink tea with milk in Paris, eat roast beef with
Yorkshire pudding in Monte Carlo, keep to one
another's company everywhere and are proud of how
cosmopolitan they have become.

In those happy days – Munich crisis or no Munich
crisis – no one really knew where Czechoslovakia was:
the problem was too small. Today we have the Bomb
of Damocles hanging over our heads, but nobody
cares: the problem is too big. In those days 'reaching
for the moon' was still a metaphor and not a short-term
programme. The 'idle rich' was still the *rentier* and not
the boilermaker on strike. We had no espresso bars,
and no rock 'n' roll. Then, the fashion was to look
forward with dismay and not to look back in anger.
After the war it seemed that we would hardly survive
the blow of victory; nonetheless, today we are nearly as

* This is a euphemism for *bloody* – a word you should never
use.

well off as the Germans themselves. We tell each other confidently that we've never had it so good but what we really mean is that we are all right, Jack.

Oh yes, if you want to be a modern Briton – a Briton of the sixties – you have to follow an entirely new set of rules. Here they follow.

G.M.

Prosperity versus *riches*

I. NEW ENGLISH

HOW TO BE PROSPEROUS

IF you want to be a modern Briton, you must be prosperous, or, preferably, rich. Richness has this in common with justice that it is not enough to be rich, you must also manifestly appear to be rich. The English, however, are a basically modest race, so you cannot just show off. In fact, you must hide your richness in an ostentatious, pseudo-modest manner, as if you were really poor. The greatest advantage of this being that you may, in fact, be really as poor as you like.

A short while back it was much more difficult to be rich, but as riches were then quite out of fashion — indeed, rather vulgar — this did not matter. A few years ago a Rolls Royce or a Bentley was a must and to have a palatial residence was advisable. Today, only the get-rich-quick businessmen, the vulgar, commercial barons and the lower layer of television comedians buy new Rollses and Bentleys. The patricians use Austin Sevens, Miniminors, scooters and bicycles, perhaps *very* ancient Rollses, or else Jensens and Bristols (the last two costing about £4,000 each but unrecognized by the masses).

It would take too long to codify the entire art of how to look prosperous and how to behave in this Age of Prosperity, but the main elementary rules are these:

1. You must get a place in the country. You remark

casually: 'Oh – we have a tumble-down old barn in Suffolk . . . ' If you can throw such a sentence away nonchalantly and especially if you learn to blush modestly while uttering it, you will unfailingly give the impression of possessing a ducal mansion on 227 acres, with thirty-four tithe cottages, eighteen liveried servants and five racing stables. Whenever I have visited the ducal mansions owned by my friends, I have invariably found dilapidated little huts where you cooked on primus stoves and where, if you needed water, you were at liberty to walk half a mile for it. You were allowed, however, to call half a mile four furlongs which sounds incomparably superior.

2. You must become amphibious and get hold of a watercraft of some sort. Here again, you must refer to 'my little launch' or even 'dinghy' with an air as though she were a yacht to put Onassis to shame. But a launch or a second-hand rubber dinghy or any superannuated rowing boat will do fine.

And it is a good idea to appear at the office – especially on Monday morning – in a dark blue blazer with shiny metal buttons; in a nautical cap instead of a bowler; and to carry in a leisurely manner and with an air of absentmindedness a sextant, an anchor and a propeller.

3. You must choose your friends with the greatest possible care. Titles are out of fashion. If you have one, keep it under your hat and in cold storage: it may come in useful again in the future. Dukes, nowadays, are not called 'Your Grace' but Bobby and Reggie; Archbishops are called 'archbish'; and second daughters of earls are spoken to as if they were ordinary human beings. Ex- and would-be debutantes are only

of use if they work in publishing houses. The most sought-after people are Greeks as there is a notion afloat that every Greek is a millionaire; Italian models (female) are also very popular; Swedes (male) are in order, if tall and very sad. Persians and foreign princes might be used in an emergency.

4. If you happen to be a butcher or a lorry driver you will be helped along the way of prosperity by periodical wins of £225,000 on the football pools. It is *de rigeur* on such occasions to declare that your win will not make the slightest difference to your way of life (after all, what does a quarter of a million matter if you already have a washing machine and a television set?), and you would not dream of giving up your £7.10.0 a week job.

5. Finally, in this Age of Prosperity you simply must play the Stock Exchange. You have to learn a few new expressions for the occasion, such as 'stock', and 'day of settlement', and 'consideration' and 'unit trust'. You must remember that your stockbroker will call the market 'easy' when it is very difficult. When reading the financial columns you must bear in mind that when the journalist says that 'steels shine today' he is using the one and only joke permitted to a poor City Editor and you'd better smile. Otherwise the very simple basic idea is that you buy shares rather cheaply, wait until they go up and up and up then sell them. It is no good to buy shares (I beg your pardon, I mean stock) at a high price and wait until they go down and down and down.

I personally do not play the Stock Exchange, because it is immoral. I lend my money, most morally, to my bank, let *them* play with it and make 120 per cent profit for themselves and pay me 2% fixed interest out of which I can pay income tax and feel a virtuous and useful member of the community.

ON TRYING TO REMAIN POOR

I T is much more difficult to try and remain poor. Indeed, one has to ask oneself: is it worth while? Let's face it: the joy has gone out of poverty.

It was soon after the war that the suddenly impoverished classes gained much in prestige. These New Poor were loud and boastful – real *nouveaux pauvres*. There was no end to their swaggering about, claiming how poor they were. As soon as you suggested a coach-trip to Hitchin or just the idea of buying a chocolate ice-cream, their eyes gleamed with pleasure and they told you with glittering pride: 'We can't afford it.' Their poverty was as ostentatious and vulgar as a gold-plated Daimler with leopard skin upholstery would be at the other pole of the financial globe, but while the display of commercial riches was *vieu jeu*, the New Poor were, at least, a new social phenomenon. Not being able to afford anything made them happy; jeering at other people's pleasures cheered them up no end. Their eyes and their trousers shone with pride.

Then the Prosperity of the early fifties descended on us and ruined it all. It took the Poor unawares and disorganized their legions. For a year or two they accepted Prosperity with a sigh. Gone were the book-keepers who dressed like bohemians; every bohemian now dressed like a book-keeper. Then, a few years after the initial blow, the revolt against respectability broke out.

The flag-bearers, the most conspicuous an ociferous *avant-garde,* were the Teddy Boys but they were not alone. Everybody who mattered protested in his own way. Filth, dirty pullovers and unshaven faces became the fashion once again; others greeted the convulsions and hoarse groans of graceless teenagers as a new art; angry young men spat at the middle classes; others, again, hurriedly exchanged their antique furniture for new and uncomfortable chairs and sofas. And a few people gave two months' holiday to their uniformed chauffeurs and went on a hitch-hiking tour in France and lived in tents.

But there was no getting away from it. That damned Prosperity had caught up with all of us. The angry young men went on spitting at the middle classes and made a tidy little fortune on the proceeds; the convulsive young singers began to shake their manes while they groaned, and that made them even richer than the angry young men; the hitch-hikers and tent-dwellers returned and money kept pouring in to all and sundry.

How to remain poor? – the worried practitioner asks himself. It is not easy. The New Poor of yesteryear are fighting a losing battle. To remain poor needs the utmost skill and ingenuity. (And only old-age pensioners and a few other unwilling people manage to achieve it – to our shame). Everything, really, is conspiring against the poor and trying to deprive them of their poverty. They had bad luck too. They moved, for example, to such districts as Islington to show how needy and destitute they were. Instead of establishing their misery, however, they managed to turn Islington into a fashionable district.

What else is left? It is no use saying that you cannot afford a car because everybody can afford a car. It is pointless to allege that you have no money because all you have to do is put your head into your bank manager's office and before you have time to say, 'Sorry, wrong room,' he will throw a couple of hundred pounds at you. (I am always puzzled why people bother to rob banks. Can't they *ask* for the money?)

How to remain poor then? I can give no foolproof recipe, only a few pointers.

1. Gambling, I believe, is almost always safe. There is no amount the horses and the dogs cannot take care of. The safest way of losing money is chasing it.

2. Try farming. It lends weary clothes-manufacturers and harassed directors of chain-stores a fresh country air, and besides it helps to get rid of any amount of money. After the war I saw a letter written by Marcel Pagnol to Sir Alexander Korda; it ran something like this (I quote from memory): 'I have discovered a truly magnificent way of losing money. It's called farming. Film-making is nothing compared with it. A film may be successful after all and you may make money on it. Never on farming. Farming is safe. You needn't worry: it will ruin you in no time.'

3. Then there is always the path of dishonesty. I mean you can always fake poverty, just in order to keep the confidence and affection of your friends. Who can prevent you from going round trying to borrow half-a-crown while you have quite a decent little nest-egg tucked away at home? Being well-off, of course, is not your shame, only your misfortune, but some people will not understand this. Alas, having money causes a great deal of discord, faction and superfluous unhappiness.

In a Soho espresso I once saw an unfortunate young man in deep despair, ostracized by his fellows because he had bought a record player and they had found out that the cheque he had given for it had not bounced.

HOW TO BE CLASS CONSCIOUS

IF you want to be a modern Englishman you must become class-conscious.

1. If you belong to the so-called higher spheres of society you will, of course, never be flagrant about this. You simply look down (not with a superior, simply with a pitying smile) upon those miserable and ridiculous creatures who do not know the conventions of your world. Nothing can possibly amuse you more than hearing someone address the third son of a marquess in the style due to the second daughter of an earl.

I must admit that I still often find these rules confusing. The other day I received an invitation to a party from a friend of mine who is a baronet. The invitation was signed by his wife – R.S.V.P. From my reference books I sought advice on how to address an envelope to a baronet's second wife. 'If the daughter of a commoner . . .' I read, then I stopped, picked up the telephone, rang the lady in question and asked her: 'I say, Eileen, are you the daughter of a commoner?'

She said: 'What the bloody hell do you mean?'

I told her: 'That will do. You are a commoner. And getting commoner and commoner every day.'

That solved that problem. Many other problems, however, still remain. One of the most exasperating cases you may come across is a Dame of the Order of

Vox Populi

the British Empire married to a baronet or a peer.
Skill, ingenuity and determination may solve even
that. But if you hear of the third daughter of a
marchioness married to an archbishop you should carefully avoid the combination.

2. Another excellent device of the British aristocracy
to drive poor foreigners – primarily Americans – crazy
is the changing of names. The fact that Lord Upper-
stone's elder son is called Lord Ipswich while his
younger son is Mr Hinch does not mean that they are
both bastards. The elder daughter of the noble Lord
may be the Hon. Mrs Cynthia Cunliffe-Green and his
younger daughter the Hon. Mary Cumberland – just
for good measure. And if even that does not drive the
poor onlooker raving mad, then the 'as he then was'
business comes in. You find such passages in field-
marshals' memoirs:

'I then went to the Viceroy's Lodge and asked to see
Lord Irwin (as he then was) without delay. I shook
Lord Halifax (as he then was not yet) by the hand in
the friendliest manner but spoke to him sternly: 'Mr
Wood,' I began, '(as he no longer was) I've just had a
message from Mr Churchill (as he then was) about 2nd
Lieutenant Birch (as he still is) etc., etc.'

3. Should you belong to any other class (except the
lower-middle – see below) you may boast of your origins
constantly. If you come from Bermondsey (or Stockton-
on-Tees or Hartley Witney) then you keep repeating
that 'the people of Bermondsey (or Stockton-on-Tees
or Hartley Witney) are the finest people in the world.'
This is just another way of saying that you, too, are one
of the finest people in the world and that you love, respect and admire yourself.

4. The one class you do *not* belong to and are not proud of at all is the lower-middle class. No one ever describes himself as belonging to the lower-middle class. Working class, yes; upper-middle class: most certainly; lower-middle class: never! Lower-middle class is, indeed, *per definitionem,* the class to which the majority of the population belongs with the exception of the few thousand people you know.

5. In the old days people used to aspire to higher classes. Since the angry young man literature has made its impact, quite a few people assert that they are of lower origin than they, in fact, are. (I am using here the word 'lower' in the worst snobbish sense.) The place of the upstart is being taken by the downstart. I know people who secretly visit evening elocution classes in order to pick up a cockney accent. Others are practising the Wigan brogue. And I know others again who would be deeply ashamed if the general public learnt that their fathers were, in fact, book-keepers and not dustmen, village grocers and not swine-herds, solicitors and not pickpockets.

THE NEW RULING CLASS

THE English talk – and talk a great deal – of upper, middle, and working classes. They also talk of upper-middle and lower-middle classes, and more recently they have started mentioning a top-working class – just to fit in between the middle-working class and the lower-middle class. This, of course, makes them fully conscious of how pitifully inadequate their language is to describe the other 120 clearly defined castes and 413 sub-castes of English society. What about the lower-middle-upper layer of the lower-upper-middle class? What about the middle-middle of the middle-middle class? And how can you really clearly distinguish between the upper-upper-middle people who by no means qualify yet for the bottom-upper?

While all this goes on, the English remain staunch believers in equality. Equality is a notion the English have given to humanity. Equality means that you are just as good as the next man but the next man is not half as good as you are.

Slowly but inescapably, however, the whole structure is being turned upside down. Oh yes, we still have an aristocracy consisting of two main branches: the old families of the peerage who look down upon the business-barons and stock-exchange-viscounts who look down upon the ancient peers. But while people still insist on sending their children to a good school (and a good school must not be confused with a school where they teach well); while for a few it is still a serious problem how to address the eldest daughter of a viscount married to an archdeacon; while some people,

Our puzzling peerage

having obtained firsts in Phoenician history at Cambridge, still expect to become directors of breweries as their birthright; while doctors and barristers are still angry that chartered accountants and actuaries should call themselves 'professional people' and while the lot of them still believe that professionals do have some prestige left – while all this still goes on the Big Businessman takes over the leading role in society with a firm hand and a quiet smile.

The great conquest by money is on. A title will not bring in money; money will bring in the title. The great fight is warming up every day. Battalions of company directors riding on the white chargers of prosperity, waving their expense accounts, their faces painted red with Burgundy, and howling their famous battle-cry: 'Long live Capital Gains!' are battering at the ancient walls of privilege. The pillars of the established order – never even cracked by the Socialists – are crumbling under their assault. Brilliant sons no longer aspire to become Lord Chancellors: they dream of controlling large advertising agencies. Soon people do not boast of being descended from a long line of generals or judges but from a long line of stockbrokers. Talent will soon mean talent to make money. A genius is one who makes a lot of money.

Soon it will come – that final take-over bid, in which Big Business will make its deadly offer to the Establishment. And if the deal goes through – as go through it will – the former people in charge will not be asked to remain at their posts.

HOW TO AVOID TRAVELLING

'TRAVEL' is the name of a modern disease which became rampant in the mid-fifties and is still spreading. The disease – its scientific name is *travelitis furiosus* – is carried by a germ called prosperity. Its symptoms are easily recognizable. The patient grows restless in the early spring and starts rushing about from one travel agent to another collecting useless information about places he does not intend to visit, studying handouts, etc.; then he, or usually she, will do a round of tailors, milliners, summer sales, sports shops, and spend three and a half times as much as he or she can afford; finally, in August, the patient will board a plane, train, coach or car and proceed to foreign parts along with thousands of fellow-sufferers not because he is interested in or attracted by the place he is bound for, nor because he can afford to go, but simply because he cannot afford not to. The disease is highly infectious. Nowadays you catch foreign travel rather as you caught influenza in the twenties, only more so.

The result is that in the summer months (and in the last few years also during the winter season) everybody is on the move. In Positano you hear no Italian but only German (for England is not the only victim of the disease); in some French parts you cannot get along unless you speak American; and the official language of the Costa Brava is English. I should not be surprised to see a notice in Blanes or Tossa de Mar stating: *Aqui Se Habla Español* – Spanish spoken here.

What is the aim of all this travelling? Each nationality has its own different one. The Americans want to take photographs of themselves in: (*a*) Trafalgar Square with the pigeons, (*b*) in St Mark's Square, Venice, with the pigeons and (*c*) in front of the Arc de Triomphe, in Paris, without pigeons. The idea is simply to collect documentary proof that *they have been there*. The German travels to check up on his guide-books: when he sees that the Ponte di Rialto is really at its proper venue, that the Leaning Tower is in its appointed place in Pisa and is leaning at the promised angle – he ticks these things off in his guide book and returns home with the gratifying feeling that he has not been swindled. But why do the English travel?

First, because their neighbour does and they have caught the bug from him. Secondly, they used to be taught that travel broadens the mind and although they have by now discovered the sad truth that whatever travel may do to the mind, Swiss or German food certainly broadens other parts of the body, the old notion still lingers on. But lastly – and perhaps mainly – they travel to avoid foreigners. Here, in our cosmopolitan England, one is always exposed to the danger of meeting all sorts of peculiar aliens. Not so on one's journeys in Europe, if one manages things intelligently. I know many English people who travel in groups, stay in hotels where even the staff is English, eat roast beef and Yorkshire pudding on Sundays and Welsh rarebit and steak and kidney pudding on weekdays, all over Europe. The main aim of the Englishman abroad is to meet people; I mean, of course, nice English people from next door or from the next street. Normally one avoids one's neighbour ('It is best to keep yourself to yourself' – 'We leave others alone and want to be left alone' etc., etc.). If you meet your next door neighbour in the High Street or at your front door you pretend not to see him or, at best, nod coolly; but if you meet him in Capri or Granada, you embrace him fondly and stand him a drink or two; and you may even discover that he is quite a nice chap after all and both of you might just as well have stayed at home in Chipping Norton.

All this, however, refers to travelling for the general public. If you want to avoid giving the unfortunate impression that you belong to the lower-middle class, you must learn *the elementary snobbery of travelling*:

1. Avoid any place frequented by others. Declare: all the hotels are full, one cannot get in anywhere. (No one will ever remark: hotels are *full of people who actually managed to get in*.)

2. Carry this a stage further and try to avoid all places interesting enough to attract other people – or, as others prefer to put it – you must get off the beaten track. In practice this means that in Italy you avoid Venice and Florence but visit a few filthy and poverty-stricken fishing villages no one has ever heard of; and if your misfortune does take you to Florence, you avoid the Uffizi Gallery and refuse to look at Michelangelo's *David*. You visit, instead, a dirty little pub on the outskirts where Tuscan food is supposed to be divine and where you can listen to a drunken and deaf accordion player.

3. The main problem is, of course, *where* to go? This is not an easy question. The *hoi polloi* may go to Paris or Spain, or the Riviera or Interlaken but such an obvious choice will certainly not do for anyone with a little self-respect. There is a small international set that leads the fashion and you must watch them. Some

years ago they discovered Capri, but now Capri is teeming with rich German and English businessmen, so you can't go near the place. Ischia became fashionable for a season or two but it too was invaded by businessmen, so Ischia is out. Majorca was next on the list, but Majorca has become quite ridiculous in the last few years: it is now an odd mixture of Munich and Oxford Street, and has nothing to offer (because needless to say, beauty and sunshine do not count). The neighbouring island of Ibiza reigned till last year but the businessmen have caught up with Ibiza too so it will stink by next summer. At the moment I may recommend Tangier; Rhodes is fairly safe too. The year after that, who knows, Capri may be tried again.

Remember: travel is supposed to make you sophisticated. When buying your souvenirs and later when most casually – you really must practise how to be casual – you refer to any foreign food, you should speak of these things in the vernacular. Even fried chicken sounds rather romantic when you speak of *Backhendl*; and you will score more points by remarking casually – very casually, I repeat – that you went to a little *Madkurve kan medbrings* near Copenhagen, than by admitting that you went to a place where you ate your own sandwiches and only ordered beer.

It is possible, however, that the mania for travelling is declining. I wonder if a Roman friend of mine was simply an eccentric or the forerunner of a new era in snobbery.

'I no longer travel at all,' he told me. 'I stay here because I want to meet my friends from all over the world.'

'What exactly do you mean?' I asked.

'It is simple,' he explained. 'Whenever I go to London, my friend Smith is sure to be in Tokyo and Brown in Sicily. If I go to Paris, Dupont is sure to be in London and Lebrun in Madagascar or Lyons. And so on. But if I stay in Rome, all my friends are absolutely sure to turn up at one time or another. The world means *people* for me. I stay here because I want to see the world.'

And he added after a short pause:

'Besides, staying at home broadens the mind.'

ON WINE SNOBBERY

A SIGNIFICANT development of the last decade is that wine-snobbery has definitely arrived in England. Before the war only a few retired scientists of University level were aware of the fact that other wines existed besides sherry and port. If you had asked (of course you never did) for wine in a pub, the publican would have taken you for a dangerous lunatic and dialled 999; today most of the pubs in Great Britain, Northern Ireland and the Channel Islands are proud to serve you 'wine per glass'.

The trouble, however, is with the wine served in restaurants. Should you, when taking a lady out to lunch, show yourself ignorant in the matter of wine, she will regard you as an unsophisticated rustic boor. It is indeed fortunate that you can get away with the most abysmally ignorant observation as long as it sounds right, because your lady-friend will know nothing about wine either. Any man who is aware that Graves is white Bordeaux, Chablis is white Burgundy, and Claret is red Bordeaux can qualify for the first

Chair of Wine Snobbery to be established at a British university. Most people know no more than that a Hock is a white Rhine wine, and are constantly astonished at the ignorance of the Germans themselves who have never heard of Hock.

Genuine expertise comes in, of course, when you begin to be able to recognize the type and the vintage of the wine served. There are two – and only two – ways of doing this: (1) Have a quick glance at the label when no one is watching. (2) Bluff.

There is no other way. I was once the guest of one of the most famous Alsatian wine-growers whose ancestors as far as he can trace were all vine-growers. I asked him if he could recognize a wine by tasting it. He said that while he would not take a Madeira for a Mâcon or his own wine for Spanish sherry, he could not be sure. Would he be able to recognize his own wine? Not necessarily, he replied. Would he be able to tell the vintage year? Well, he said, there were certain very characteristic years and he would not mix up, say, a 1952 wine with a 1948 – but, apart from typical cases, he could not be sure. Wine of the same vintage may differ according to what side of the hill it comes from; and even bottles coming from the same barrel may taste different to the expert. What can the poor amateur wine-snob do then? You cannot possibly nod all the time when the waiter pours out wine for you and asks you to taste it. A low constant murmur of approval merely gives the impression that you are no connoisseur of wine, and that is more than any self-respecting Englishman can bear nowadays. I can give you three important tips in this field. But whichever you may choose (and all three may be tried on suc-

An impertinent little Margaux

cessive occasions) you must first practise at home. You must, first of all, learn the names of a few famous wines (Traminer, Ribeauville, Pouilly-Fuissé, etc.) and you must also learn what goes with what when ordering. There was one school which tried to be terribly broad-minded by ordering, say, red Burgundy with fish, accompanied by the exclamation: 'I am broad-minded, I just take what I like' – but this is on the decline and not recommended. Your lady-companion may be worried lest people at the next table, unaware that you are being broad-minded, may regard you as an ignorant lout. I should mention here that while you are studying the wine list, your lady-friend may come up with a helpful suggestion. She may say:

'Oh, we had a wonderful Herriko-Arnoa in the Basque country. Please, Jack, order Herriko-Arnoa.'

The answer in such cases is this:

'Herriko-Arnoa is indeed a magnificent wine. But I am afraid it *does not travel well.*'

A man who knows how various wines travel is simply irresistible. But to return to your homework: you must practise at home, putting a little wine in your mouth and making it travel around inside your mouth while you adopt a meditative, pensive expression. Without this expression the whole show is worthless; any answer thrown out without gargling or looking thoughtful, gives you away as a dilettante. And after gargling, you may say one of four things:

1. In the case of white wine you may always say – very thoughtfully – that it is not cold enough. This is not too witty or too original but it is better than nothing. Incomparably better than nodding feebly and not criticizing at all.

2. In the case of red wine, you say: 'It is not *chambré* enough.' With a little bit of luck your lady-friend will not know what *chambré* means. But even if she does, the phrase is still magnificent.

3. A brand new device – a variation on the theme: you click your tongue with irritation and send back a bottle of white wine because it is *too cold,* red because it is *too chambré.* (It is amazing how long it took to think up that one.)

4. This version is the *pièce de résistance;* it is to be used only on rare occasions when the impression you wish to make is of decisive importance. You gargle with the wine, go into a species of coma and then declare – more to yourself than to the lady:

'This comes from the sunny side of the hill ... '

The remark is known to have turned the heads of the haughtiest and least impressionable of women.

Wine snobbery, by the way, is unknown on the Continent. There you find whisky, gin, and dry Martini snobberies, in turn, or – this is the latest – beer snobbery in Italy. A friend of mine – a Frenchman with a considerable reputation as a lady-killer – told me once that nowadays he offers a little wine and plenty of *cognac* to his lady-friends. He sighed and remarked: 'I used to say it with flowers ... More gallant, no doubt ... But with *cognac* it is so much quicker.'

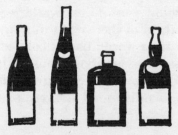

ON SHOPPING

MY greatest difficulty in turning myself into a true Britisher was the Art of Shopping. In my silly and primitive Continental way, I believed that the aim of shopping was to *buy* things; to buy things, moreover, you needed or fancied. Today I know that (*a*) shopping is a social – as opposed to a commercial – activity and (*b*) its aim is to help the shopkeeper to get rid of all that junk.

Shopping begins with queueing. If you want to become a true Briton, you must still be fond of queueing. An erstwhile war-time necessity has become a national entertainment. Just as the Latins need an opportunity of going berserk every now and then in order to let off steam, so the British are in need of certain excesses, certain wild bouts of self-discipline. A man in a queue is a fair man; he is minding his own business; he lives and lets live; he gives the other fellow a chance; he practises a duty while waiting to practise his own rights; he does almost everything an Englishman believes in doing. A man in a queue is as much the image of a true Briton as a man in a bull-ring is the image of a Spaniard or a man with a two-foot cigar of an American.

When your turn comes at last in the shop, disregard the queue behind you. They would feel let down if you deprived them of their right to wait and be virtuous. Do not utter a word about the goods you wish to buy. Ask the shopkeeper about his health, his wife, his children, his dogs, cats, goldfish, and budgerigars; his holiday plans, his discarded holiday plans and about his last two or three holidays; his views on the weather, the test match; discuss the topical and more entertaining murder cases, etc., etc., and, naturally answer all *his* questions.

A few further rules for true Britons:

1. Never criticize anybody's wares, still less return anything to the shop if it turns out to be faulty, rotten or falling to bits. Not only might this embarrass the shopkeeper but it might also infringe one of the fundamental civil rights of all Englishmen, secured in Magna Carta: to sell rubbish to the public. This system has its own impenetrable logic. With tailors, dressmakers and hairdressers you may be as unreasonable as you choose. But to give back a singularly thick piece of meat to a butcher when you have asked for a singularly thin one is fussing. To insist on records of *Aïda*, failing to be content with *Tristan and Isolde* or *The Mikado* instead (when the dealer has made it clear that he would rather get rid of these two) is extremely un-English. Milder and truer types of Britons are known to have bought typewriters ·instead of tape-recorders, bubble-cars instead of bedroom suites and grand pianos instead of going to the Costa Brava for their holidays.

2. Always be polite to shop assistants. Never talk back to them; never argue; never speak to them unless spoken to. If they are curt, sarcastic or rude to you, remember that they might be in a bad mood.

3. If there happens to be no queue in a shop when you arrive, never be impatient if no one takes the slightest notice of you. Do not disturb the assistants in their *tête-à-tête;* never disturb the one who stands in the corner gazing at you with bemused curiosity. There is nothing personal in the fact that they ignore

you: they are simply Miltonists. All English shop assistants are Miltonists. A Miltonist firmly believes that 'they also serve who only stand and wait.'

HOW TO SAVE THE WORLD

ONLY one shortage in England survived the Seven (or was it Fourteen?) Lean Years: the shortage of Good Causes. When I first came to this country, there were plenty of serious problems to get excited about: Nazi-ism, Fascism, Appeasement, the Spanish Civil War, etc. What is left of all these? Nothing – absolutely nothing.

Anti-Communism has been played out. Even the ex-Communists have nothing left to say. Besides, Mr Krushchev passes nowadays as the favourite clown of the free world – such a witty, jovial old boy. *Because* he has a sense of humour, the English (those incomparable champions of the *non sequitur*) are convinced that he is a dear old-fashioned liberal. If only he had not fired that poor little dog Laika into space, he might have successfully claimed to be elected Chancellor of Oxford University.

It is true that we have some minor issues left on our hands, such as nuclear disarmament, South African apartheid, Notting Hill, Little Rock, swastika daubings and such like, but apart from a few dotty intellectuals no one gets really worked up about these. All this is a great pity, because ways and means of fighting for good causes (or for bad ones) have improved beyond recognition.

Take for example nuclear disarmament. Are you

*The World's favourite Clown, or the life and soul of the
Party*

for or against blowing up our planet with hydrogen bombs? According to the Public Opinion Polls. 2·2% are for it, 1·7% are against it and the rest (96·1%) don't know. Suppose you yourself are against it and you are convinced that the best way to secure our safety is to destroy our own bombs, persuade the Americans to do the same and put our loyal trust in Mr Nikita Krushchev, that dear old liberal (but for that dog, Laika). You may write a very excellent and persuasive book on the subject: it will be reviewed at length in the quality newspapers and political weeklies – in other words, it will remain unnoticed; you may lecture about your ideas to this or that learned society; you may form a club or a party to propagate your thesis; you may hold mass meetings in Caxton Hall – no one will blink an eyelid. But should you, along with a few of your followers, lie down in front of the main gateway at Harwell so that the police have to remove you, you will then be front page news all over the world. Should your disciples do their act in top-hats, pictorial coverage will be quite superb – indeed, you will practically monopolize television news bulletins and other news features for three days.

Here I give you some elementary advice on how to propagate good or bad causes:

1. If you have discovered a wonderful new dietary system which might benefit humanity to no small degree, do not bother about the *Lancet* or the *British Medical Journal;* forget about scientific institutions. All you have to do is walk from John o'Groats to Land's End. Thousands will come out to cheer you, traffic will stop when you pass through a town and you will become a national figure whether you like it or not, how-

ever shy you may be, and however honest and noble your original intentions may have been. Your advice and views will henceforth be sought on every question under the sun (with the simple exception of dietetics).

2. If you believe in the old glories of the Empire, all you have to do is to go to other people's meetings, wave rattles, make cat-calls and blow horns. If that does not convince the world that your ideas on the Empire are sound, nothing will.

3. If, as a poet of genius, you are dissatisfied with selling four poems a year and living on a total annual income of £3.12.6, your course of action is clear. Grow a picturesque beard, put on a purple robe, prepare two sandwich-boards for yourself, stating: STARVING POET and FAIR DEAL FOR GENIUSES! and start selling your poems, printed on pillow-cases, in front of a church where a top social wedding is just being solemnized. Your future will be safe. Your poems will be in such demand that you will not be able to turn out enough of the stuff. You will make millions and will continue to be revered as the 'Starving Bard in Purple'.

4. Generally speaking, organize mass marches, wave banners and sell your memoirs on the slightest provocation. You may kill someone and – with a little bit of luck – your crime may pass practically unnoticed in the press, but should you refuse to pay a £1 parking fine and go to prison for your principles (if any) you will find that your publicity will far outdo anything attained by the late Dr Crippen. Suppose you have really hit upon the Word, that you have seen the Light and can at last give us the Creed to save erring humanity, all you have to do is go and dance a cha-cha-cha

SOCIETY FOR THE
SUPPRESSION OF
PRACTICALLY
EVERYTHING

in your bare feet for an hour or two in front of the House of Lords, wearing a turban. The victory of your ideas is assured.

HOW TO BE FREE

THE modern Englishman is jealous of his civil liberties and rightly so. Modern freedom is an English invention – or at least an excellent English adaptation of the original Greek. The ancient and essential liberties are well known to us all; here I only want to say a few words on the new interpretation of some old ideas:

1. FREEDOM OF SPEECH. You may say whatever you like *as long as you circulate in one copy only*. You may go to Hyde Park and say whatever you fancy (with certain exceptions) as long as you do not appear in duplicate and are not mass-produced in any shape or form. This is called Freedom of Speech. The trouble is that it may seem a little hard to rouse millions by delivering speeches, however eloquent they may be, in Hyde Park. To make any real impact you would need the Freedom of the *Daily Express* or the Freedom of Independent Television. But as none of us (including the *Daily Express* or Independent or B.B.C. Television has anything of shattering importance to say just now, you might as well stick to Hyde Park.

Modern traffic has produced a number of new freedoms, unlisted in the old statutes:

2. THE FREEDOM OF JAY-WALKING. Englishmen in cars are prepared up to a point to obey traffic signals; but the very idea that an English pedestrian should

wait for the green light is absolutely outrageous. The Englishman's right to walk under the wheels of lorries was secured in Magna Carta and ours is not the generation to squander such ancient liberties.

3. THE RIGHT TO REFUSE BLOOD-TESTS – or breathing tests – is another basic right. in fact, you often hear people *defending themselves* by saying that they only had three whiskies, eight gins and five pints of beer. Anyone who tries to deprive Englishmen of their right to kill on the road is far worse than a tyrant: he is a spoil-sport.

4. Zebra crossings have produced a peculiar new type of mentality in an increasing number of people. This has its new correlated freedom: THE RIGHT TO ZEBRA-CROSS. If Freud were still alive he would certainly be able to define this new psychological trait, this zebra-complex. For those afflicted, life is simply a huge zebra-crossing: as soon as they step into the arena they expect all movement to come to a standstill and give way to them. In very bad cases the patient expects people to watch him admiringly and wave to him with friendly smiles.

IN PRAISE OF TELEVISION

WHEN I first came to England, television was still a kind of entertainment and not a national disease. During the happy war years it was off the air altogether but afterwards it returned with a vengeance.

In the early post-war period, television drew a peculiar dividing line in society. While people boasted wildly of not being able to afford a half of bitter or a pair of new shoelaces, they always *refused* to have television sets. No one ever admitted that he could not afford one. You 'cannot afford' to fulfil a dream; but a television set was rejected on its merits as something belonging to the lower orders. The English middle class were as proud of not possessing television sets as they are of not knowing foreign languages.

Television, however, has slowly conquered – in varying degree – all layers of society and, whether we like it or not – it has come to stay.

I have watched a large number of programmes from the nadir of most variety shows up to the upper-middle-brow *Monitor*. I have watched innumerable statesmen boarding and leaving aeroplanes with heavy, meaningful faces and have always been astonished to find that the same platitudes can be expressed in so many different ways. During our periodically recurrent strikes, I have listened to trade union leaders and employers on Mondays and was impressed to learn that no concessions could be made in matters of principle; only to be told on Wednesdays that their relinquishing of these principles was – on *their* part – victory for common sense and a true service to the community. I have heard innumerable party politicians explaining that defeat is victory, and that it is high time to save civilization by restoring hanging, birching and flogging. I am always fascinated at the sight of mild, slightly bewildered people putting up with the insolent and aggressive questions of those interviewers who button-hole them in the street or drag them into a studio. I like the Brains Trust, too – its poets and interior decorators with the gift of the gab, who are able to utter weighty opinions on every subject under the sun without a moment's reflection. I am fond of watching people in Tanganyika or Madagascar catching rats, snakes and worms for pets while black ladies with bare bosoms look on. (Personally, I should like black ladies with bare bosoms to appear in all my programmes.)

The basis and main pillar of the art of television is the TELEVISION PERSONALITY. If you want to become a Television Personality, you need a personality of some sort. It may be unattractive or simply repulsive; but a personality is indispensable.

On the whole I like television very much indeed. The reasons for my devotion are these:

1. Television is one of the chief architects of prosperity. Certain television personalities can give away money with great charm on the slightest provocation. It is their habit – indeed, their second nature – to give you a refrigerator or a motor-scooter if you happen to pass near them. Should you chance to know what the capital of France is called, or who our war-time Prime Minister was with the initials of W.S.C. – if you are able to scratch your left ear with your right foot while lying on the floor blindfold and watched by ten million giggling spectators, then you are practically certain

'. . . no concessions
must be made.'

'. . . must be a cer-
tain amount of give
and take.'

'. . . look forward to
an era of increasing
stability.'

'. . . we are living in
a topsy-turvy world.'

to be sent to Majorca for a three weeks' holiday. If you can tell whether *polygamy* is something to eat or something you find in coconut trees, or recognize the features of a fourth-rate comedian or fifth-rate guitarist in *Dotto*, you are almost bound to get an annuity for life.

2. Television is also one of the main architects of slumps. A short while ago *Panorama* made a report on the stock-exchange boom, in the course of which one or two people made some cautious remarks about the boom not lasting forever, and recalled the Wall Street crash when people threw themselves out of the windows of skyscrapers. Next day hordes of people sold their shares, thus causing a fall unknown since the days of the Suez crisis. The bank rate had to be raised three days later and if *Dotto* and a few other programmes had not rectified the country's economic balance by giving away even more washing-machines, bubble-cars and tea-sets, we would have faced utter and irretrievable ruin.

3. Television has united the family – by keeping the family at home, gaping at it round the family hearth.

4. Television causes more friction in family life than any other single factor by offering unique scope for quarrels as to which programme to watch.

5. Television is of great educational value. It teaches you while still really young how to (*a*) kill, (*b*) rob, (*c*) embezzle, (*d*) shoot (*e*) poison, and generally speaking, (*f*) how to grow up into a Wild West outlaw or gangster by the time you leave school.

6. Television puts a stop to crime because all the burglars and robbers, instead of going to burgle and

rob, sit at home watching *The Lone Ranger, Emergency Ward Ten* and *Dotto*.

7. Television has undeniably raised the general level of culture throughout the country. Some people allege that it has killed the habit of reading and thinking – but there is no truth in this. I have yet to meet a person who gave up his methodical study of, say, early Etruscan civilization in order to be able to watch more of *Sunday Night at the London Palladium* or who has stopped reading Proust or Plutarch because he could not tear himself away from *What's My Line?* or *Spot the Tune*. I believe that in most cases the devotees are better off watching *Army Game* than listening to one another's conversation. And this brings me to my last point – overleaf.

Weather Report

ON THE ART OF CONVERSATION

THE main and the most glorious achievement of television is that it is killing the art of conversation. If we think of the type of conversation television is helping to kill, our gratitude must be undying. The trouble is that it has not yet killed enough of it. Some of it is still alive and flourishing in Britain.

A few days ago I was observing two sisters and their brother at a seaside resort. The sisters – around sixty years of age – lived at Bexhill and their brother, a few years younger, at Folkestone. These three – because of the great distances involved, amounting to something like fifty miles – had not met for over ten years. The reunion was a happy and uproarious occasion. They had so much to tell each other that they often stayed up chatting till after midnight. I could not help overhearing a great deal of their conversation. It went like this:

BROTHER: It struck me when I was out before supper, that the wind is going round to the south . . .

ITS SISTER: Yes . . . definitely. What do you think, Muriel?

MURIEL: I couldn't agree with you more. Yes. Southerly. Definitely. Yes.

BROTHER: I don't like south winds. Not in these parts. Do *you*, Grace?

GRACE: Oh no . . . Heaven forbid. No south winds for me. Not in these parts. What do you think, Muriel?

MURIEL: I couldn't agree with you more. No south winds.

No, thank you. Oh no. No, no, no.

BROTHER: Get a lot of south winds at Bexhill, Grace?

GRACE: Not a lot. A fair amount. We get our fair share of south winds. You know how it is. One has to take the rough with the smooth.

BROTHER: I like west winds, personally. West winds are fun.

GRACE: Oh yes. I do enjoy a good west wind. We often get west winds at Bexhill, don't we, Muriel?

MURIEL: Fair amount. I couldn't agree with you more. Not too much though. But we mustn't complain, must we?

GRACE: No.

BROTHER: Yes.

GRACE: Yes.

MURIEL: Oh yes . . . definitely. I couldn't agree with you more.

GRACE: No.

BROTHER: Oh no.

MURIEL: Yes.

And so on, and so on. I listened for another hour or two, then I jumped up, went to the television set and shouted:

'I am thirsty for the pleasures of the pure intellect! *Dotto* for me!'

ON ADVERTISEMENTS

ALL advertisements – particularly television advertisements – are utterly and hopelessly un-English. They are too outspoken, too definite, too boastful. Why not evolve a national British style in television advertising instead of slavishly imitating the American style of breathless superlatives, with all their silly implications (buy our shampoo and you'll get a husband; buy our perfume and you are sure to be attacked by hungry males in Bond Street; smoke our pipe-tobacco and you will become a sun-tanned Adonis)? I feel sure that the effect of these advertisements could be vastly improved if they were made more English. Some ads, for example, could be given an undertone of gambling:

GRAPIREX: It may relieve your headache. Or, of course, it may not. Who can tell? Try it. You may be lucky. The odds against you are only 3 to 1.

Or:

Try your luck on BUMPEX Fruit Juice. Most people detest it. You may be an exception.

Or appeal to the Englishman's sense of fairness. A beautiful, half-nude girl (you cannot do without them in any advertisement, British, American or anything else) might call to the public:

S.O.S. We are doing badly. Business is rotten. Buy Edgeless Razor Blades and give us a sporting chance. Honestly, they're not much worse than other makes.

Or appeal to the Englishman's inborn honesty:

Use BUBU Washing Powder. By the way, have you ever tried the *whiteness* test? Here is Mrs Spooner from Framlingham. Now, Mrs Spooner, which would you say is the whiter of these two pairs of knickers?
MRS SPOONER: This one.
ANNOUNCER: You are perfectly right, Mrs Spooner. That is the one washed in PRIDE. So you don't get your five pounds, Mrs Spooner – no fear. Nevertheless, ladies and gentlemen, just go on using BUBU. Who likes that blinding, ugly, vulgar whiteness, in any case? After all, people don't see your knickers. At least they shouldn't. BUBU WASHES GREYEST.

Or, just moderate your language. Make no extravagant claims; be vague and incoherent; in other words natural.

CRANFIELD chocolate is rather nourishing. Never mind the taste.

Or:

Drink DANFORD'S beer. It's dirt cheap and you CAN get used to it.

Or else:

Can you tell the difference between our margarine and our hair tonic? WE can't.

ON POLITICS

THE fundamental concept of British political life is the two-party system. The essence of the two-party system is that there are either 358 parties or one; but never, in any circumstances, are there two. To explain: both parties reflect such a vast spectrum of opinion from left to right that the left wings of both parties are poles apart from their right wings and in no other country would politicians ideologically so remote from each other even dream of belonging to the same political organizations. In the two main parties – with the Liberals thrown in for good measure – there is enough raw material – I have just checked it again – for $358\frac{1}{2}$ parties. (The half being a minor group which advocates the nationalization of the button-manufacturing industry in so far as it consists of firms employing more than 33·7 workers. The ·7 of a worker is, of course, on part-time.)

Or else, as I have mentioned, you may say that while the Labour Party has a few real leftists and the Tories a few real rightists (and vice versa), the rest of the two parties simply overlap and one single party would do quite adequately instead of two. In many cases it is really just a toss-up whether Mr X or Mr Y joins this party or that. To cross and recross the floor of the House is not unheard-of; it does not necessarily ruin your chances within your own party. Sir Winston Churchill, for example, managed reasonably well in the Conservative Party after his temporary absence in the ranks of their rivals. (There is nothing illogical in this. My whole point is: in most cases it does not really matter which party you belong to.)

The period after 1945 was exceptional. Then the Labour Party really had a programme (I personally believe an admirable one) and carried it out. The trouble was that they did not have *enough* programme and used up the little they had too quickly. Then they started scratching their heads in embarrassment: what to do next? While scratching, they fell from power and then a 1066-ish period started for them. I do not refer to the actual period of the Norman conquest; I refer to the book *1066 and All That*. A violent dispute ensued (on various levels of intelligence and literacy) on whether nationalization was a Good Thing or a Bad Thing. Whether it was better to be Leftist than to be in Power? Whether a change to a Tory programme would ensure, at last, a Labour victory?

While dispute is still raging and while some Socialists are still trying to convince one another that their leader would be more at home in the Tory Party, the Tories are carrying on a normal and by no means extremist Socialist policy. They speak of the blessings of the Welfare State as if they had not opposed it tooth and nail; they assure us in all their manifestos that they are doing more for the poor, the old-age pensioners, the down-trodden, the workers, the underdog and even now and then for the overdogs such as the landlords, than Labour ever did. In other words, they are riding on the crest of world prosperity – and they are pretty good riders.

And while the Tories are trying to establish a mild, non-Marxist, faintly paternal Socialist regime, the

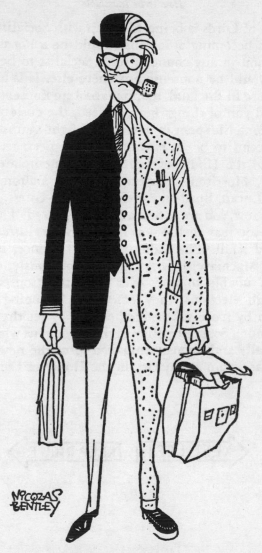

The Two-Party System

House of Lords is being filled up with Socialist peers. A lord becoming a Socialist would be a normal phenomenon in any country; for a Socialist to become a lord would be nonsense anywhere else. It is absolute nonsense in England, too, but absolute nonsense is the normal run of things here. Indeed, the customary reward for a life spent in determined fight against privilege, seems to be an elevation to the peerage. If you go into the House of Lords and contemplate Lords Attlee, Morrison, Alexander, Silkin, Dalton, Shawcross, Lucan, Burden, Kershaw, Haden-Guest, etc., all in one row, you are at first a little perplexed. Then suddenly you may realize – as I did – the devilish pattern behind it all. The Labour Party, for once, is being really Machiavellian. As they are obviously, or so it seems, unable to take over from the Conservatives through elections, they enforce a Changing of the Guard by more subtle methods: they let the Tories carry out a Socialist policy in the Commons while they gradually and almost unnoticed form the new aristocracy and gain a majority in the House of Lords.

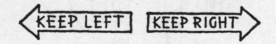

HOW TO STOP ROAD TRAFFIC

THE greatest change in my twenty-one years is the
way Britain has become motorized. When I first came
only a rich person could afford a car; today only a rich
person can afford to be without one.

This motorization has developed into a war between
the motorists and the authorities. A feature of other
wars is mobilization; the main feature of this one is
immobilization.

The conduct of the war itself clearly reflects British
genius at its best. The authorities were quick enough
to discover that cars are a menace and a nuisance and
should be stopped at all costs. So the Police, the
Ministry of Transport, local authorities and quite a
few other bodies joined forces to form a secret society
under the name of the Royal Society for the Prevention
of Motor Transport.

Each constituent body of the R.S.P.M.T. has its own
function in the society's stratagem. The general idea
is to make roads and streets impassable and bring
traffic to a standstill in the shortest possible time and
thus free us from the danger of motor traffic for ever.
The Ministry of Transport's job is to deprive the
country not only of motorways – as is generally believed
– but of *all sorts of roads*. This aim is achieved by the
devices known as (1) road-building, (2) road repairs and
(3) improving the Highway Code which is, in fact, a
clever way of spreading confusion.

1. The Minister of Standstill – as he is commonly
referred to in R.S.P.M.T. circles – in spite of occasional
flurries of activity and waves of self-advertisement –

has various means at his disposal for preventing road-building. The laws of the land are, of course, of the utmost help; also the administrative methods: several hundred local authorities can cause larger and healthier confusion than the Ministry could by its own unaided efforts, efficient though the Ministry is.

Everyone in England is clamouring for more roads through the other fellow's land and skirting other people's towns – your own land and immediate neighbourhood being, of course, sacred and exempt.

So the first seven years of any road-building programme are taken up with appeals against the plan by those who desperately want more roads. If, in spite of its efforts, the Ministry cannot prevent the sporadic conclusion of a small stretch of motorway here and there, it need not lose heart. To accept defeat would not be the British way. There are two main methods of retaliation:

a. If, in spite of every effort, a stretch of motorway is actually opened, it should be closed again as soon after the ceremonial opening as political considerations permit;

b. if you cannot prevent traffic on the motorway itself, block it at the entrances and exits.

2. Road repair is an even more effective way of driving motorists insane. Under the excuse of 'keeping the road in good repair', half the roads and streets of England may be constantly blocked, closed, halved, quartered, made one-way, etc. A secret order of the Ministry of Standstill reads:

Inasmuch as after seven or eight years of strenuous work, minor road-repairs must unfortunately be terminated, the cooperation of the local authorities is now sought. As soon as the road is covered by the new asphalt, but before it dries it is to be torn up again by the gas authorities; the same procedure is to be repeated by the Water Board authorities; by telephone linesmen; by the Sanitary authorities; by the Inland Revenue; by the local education authorities; by the Chelsea Pensioners. As soon as the last-named body has completed operations, ordinary road-repairs may safely recommence.

3. Another trick of the Minister of Standstill is to spread confusion, alarm and despondency among the ranks of motorists. Not long ago, for example, the Minister decided to *clarify* the rules of priority on the roundabouts.

He decreed: *there are no rules of priority on the roundabouts*. It is as simple as that. It is a strict rule that there is no rule. Having made this clear to everyone once and for all, he abolished the 'overtake me' signal, adding in a statement that he hoped motorists would go on using it.

4. The Police are responsible for inventing that sublime doctrine: *cars should move but never stop*. The Police are perfectly right, of course. You do not need an expensive motor vehicle down in the street if you are up in an office. In fact, if you want to *stay* somewhere, you do not need a car at all. The most heinous offence known to the Police is officially called 'obstructing the Queen's Highway'. The Queen is brought into it to underline the close connection between a parking offence and high treason.

The Police insist—as full members of the R.S.P.M.T.

should – that taxis should always pick up and put down passengers in the middle of the streets and stop there without signals. And they dote on their main hench-men, the refuse-lorries, and work out complicated pat-terns for them to ensure that these Refuse Collecting Vehicles (as they are fondly called) and their happy crews should block the largest number of streets for the longest possible time. They encourage double parking, dangerous parking, careless parking everywhere but they may tow away your car from a peaceful suburban street just to show that they have the Public Good at heart.

5. Parking rules – whether in the temporary Pink Zone or outside – is one of those mysterious English ways a foreigner will never understand.

a. There are streets (in Soho, for example) where parking is absolutely and totally prohibited during the daytime. These streets are chock-full of cars all down one side. If the other side fills up too, that is all right. The 'total prohibition' was only a joke.

b. Most High Streets all over the country are filled with the cars of the shopkeepers and their assistants from 9 a.m. to 6.30 p.m. If delivery vans or customers want to park, they must – and indeed do – double park. The streets become first dangerous, then impassable. The police wink a benevolent eye at this. After all, it is only fair that the British shopkeeper should try to keep customers away from his shop by barricading his entrance with his own car; and it is equally fair that the customer should not take such an attitude lying down.

c. Secrets, generally speaking, are not very well kept nowadays. With reporters and television cameras all

An executive officer of the Royal Society for the Prevention of Motor Transport must be ready for action at any time . . .

round us, the secrets of conference chambers, however
well guarded, become public knowledge in no time.
There can be no doubt that the best kept secret in England is: where one can park a car and where not. Not
even the Lord Chief Justice of England can be sure
about that. The law is this: parking is allowed, really,
everywhere; 'causing obstruction' is strictly prohibited
everywhere. But parking is defined as causing obstruction; consequently it is allowed and prohibited at the
same time, everywhere. Just another triumph of that
clear English way of thinking which – I believe – they
are fond of calling empirical.

Many people believe that the motorization of the
land has greatly changed the British character. A member of the Government has recently declared that as
soon as an ordinary Briton touches the steering wheel
he reverts to a savage cave-man. This, I feel, is an empty
boast on the Minister's part. I have driven cars in New
York, Paris, Rome and Tokyo as well as in London and
I am certain that while the British, no doubt, have
their fair share of road-hogs, neurotics and incompe-
tent asses among their drivers, on the whole they are
the most courteous and civilized of all motoring
nations. Personally, I am used to French driving and
like it; but most Britons regard an English Bank Holiday jam as a sheer joy-ride compared with a normal,
week-day drive round the Arc de Triomphe. But the
French, in turn, are still the incarnation of tact, old-
world chivalry and timidity compared with the Japanese. Why then do ministers boast of our rudeness on
the roads? Why do drivers regard their fellow-drivers
(commonly referred to as 'the other idiot') as cave-men
and barbarians? Simply because, deep in the English

soul, there is a deep-seated desire and a passionate long-
ing to be rude. Rudeness is one of the admired and
coveted vices of virility. I know that whenever I call
an Englishman rude he takes it as a compliment; by
now I have learnt to call people rude only when I want
to flatter them. Yet the English are fighting a losing
battle. With an effort they may manage to be silly, lazy,
indolent, selfish, and obstinate; now and then they may
even manage to be cruel. But rude? Never.

II. OLD ENGLISH

HOW TO TAKE YOUR PLEASURE SADLY

I DO not know how the silly phrase 'the English take their pleasures sadly' originated. Slavs take their pleasures sadly. A Russian cannot really enjoy himself without sobbing for an hour or two on another Slavonic bosom. But Englishmen? They, in their moments of pleasure, may be unemotional, shy, phlegmatic – but sad? Oh no, not sad.

The English, instead of taking their pleasures sadly, endure them bravely, in a spirit worthy of their Puritan ancestors. I often imagine a modern Grand Inquisitor summoning an Englishman and sending him on a normal summer holiday. He pronounces sentence:

'One: tomorrow morning you will get into your car and take twelve and a half hours to cover a four-hour journey. The journey back will take you fifteen hours and the fumes will nearly choke you.

'Two: when you reach your destination, you will queue up twelve times a day: three times for ice-cream, twice for deck-chairs, three times for beer, once for tea, twice for swings for the children and once just for the hell of it.

'Three: whenever you feel unbearably hot, I order you to accept the additional torture of drinking hot tea.

'Four: when it gets still hotter, you will drive down

*May it please thee, O Lord, to grant that thy humble
servant shall submit to whatsoever earthly pleasures shall
afflict him with grace and forebearance worthy of thy
Holy name . . .*

to the seaside and sit in the oven of your car, for two hours and a half.

'Five: wherever you go, there will never be less than two thousand people around you. They will shout and shriek into your ear and trample on your feet and your only consolation will be that you, too, trample on *their* feet. There is no escape from them. You may try the countryside but the countryside, too, will be transformed into an ever-lasting Bank Holiday fairground, strewn with paper bags and empty tins and bottles. Furthermore, to add to your sufferings, I order you to take a portable radio everywhere with you and listen to 'Housewives' Choice' and 'Mrs Dale's Diary' incessantly!'

If all this were meted out as dire punishment, proud, free Englishmen everywhere would rise against it as they have always risen against foul oppression. But as, on top of it all, they have to spend a whole year's savings on these pleasures, they are delighted if they can join the devotees anywhere.

Britain has been the marvel-country of the world for a long time. Many people used to regard her as decadent, decaying and exhausted until they learned better. How has Britain come out of her many trials, not only victorious but rejuvenated? The secret of the British is very simple: if they can endure their summer holidays, they can endure anything.

ON NOT KNOWING ENGLISH

I THINK it is vital that I give some instructions concerning the English language. I cannot do better than to repeat – with slight alterations –what I have said on this subject before.*

When I was sent to England in 1938 I thought I knew English fairly well. In Budapest my English proved quite sufficient. I could get along with it. On arrival in this country, I found that Budapest English was quite different from London English. I should not like to seem biased, but I found Budapest English much better in many ways.

In England I found two difficulties. First: I did not understand people, and secondly: they did not understand me. It was easier with written texts. Whenever I read a leading article in *The Times*, I understood everything perfectly well, except that I could never make out whether *The Times* was for or against something. In those days I put this down to my lack of knowledge of English.

The first step in my progress was when people started understanding me while I still could not understand them. This was the most talkative period of my life. Trying to hide my shortcomings, I went on talking, keeping the conversation as unilateral as possible. I reached the stage of intelligibility fairly quickly, thanks to a friend of mine who discovered an important linguistic secret, namely that the English mutter and mumble. Once we noticed a sausage-like thing in a

* *Shakespeare and Myself*, George Mikes. Drawings by David Langdon. André Deutsch, 8s. 6d. Order your copy *now*.

'*Can't you understand plain English?*'

shop window marked PORK BRAWN. We mistook it for a Continental kind of sausage and decided to buy some for our supper. We entered the shop and I said: 'A quarter of pork brawn please.' 'What was that?' asked the shopkeeper looking scared. 'A quarter of pork brawn, please,' I repeated, still with a certain nonchalance. I repeated it again. I repeated it a dozen times with no success. I talked slowly and softly; I shouted; I talked in the way one talks to the mentally deficient; I talked as one talks to the deaf and finally I tried baby-talk. The shopkeeper still had no idea whether we wanted to buy or sell something. Then my friend had a brain-wave. 'Leave it to me,' he said in Hungarian and started mumbling under his nose in a hardly audible and quite unintelligible manner. The shopkeeper's eyes lit up: 'I see,' he said happily, 'you want a quarter of pork brawn. Why didn't you say so?'

The next stage was that I began to understand foreigners but not the English or the Americans. The more atrocious a foreign accent someone had, the clearer he sounded to me.

But time passed and my knowledge and understanding of English grew slowly. Until the time came when I began to be very proud of my knowledge of English. Luckily, every now and then one goes through a sobering experience which teaches one to be more humble. Some years ago my mother came here from Hungary on a visit. She expressed her wish to take English lessons at an L.C.C. class, which some of her friends attended. I accompanied her to the school and we were received by a commissionaire. I enquired about the various classes and said that we were interested in the class for beginners. I received all the necessary information and conducted a lengthy conversation with the man, in the belief that my English sounded vigorous and idiomatic. Finally, I paid the fees for my mother. He looked at me with astonishment and asked: 'Only for one? And what about you?'

ON NOT KNOWING FOREIGN LANGUAGES

A TRUE-BORN Englishman does not know any language. He does not speak English too well either but, at least, he is not proud of this. He is, however, immensely proud of not knowing any foreign languages. Indeed, inability to speak foreign languages seems to be the major, if not the only, intellectual achievement of the average Englishman.

1. If you, gentle reader, happen to be an alien and are in the process of turning yourself into a proper Briton, you must get rid of your knowledge of *all* foreign languages. As this includes your own mother tongue, the task does not seem an easy one. But do not lose heart. Quite a few ex-aliens may proudly boast of having succeeded in forgetting their mother tongue without learning English.

2. If you are an Englishman, you must not forget that the way foreigners speak English is an endless source of hilarity and mirth. It is not funny that you yourself may have been living in Stockholm, Winterthur or Lahore for forty-three years without picking up even broken Swedish or Schwitzerdütsch or even pidgin Punjabi; it is on the other hand always excruciatingly funny if an English-speaking taxi-driver in

English as she is spoke

Lima splits his infinitives or a news-vendor in Oberammergau uses an unattached participle.

3. If you – in spite of all precautions – cannot help picking up a foreign language or two (sometimes it is in the air and you catch it as you catch flu) – then you *always* refer to the language you know as Italian, Spanish, Japanese, etc. A language you do not know at all should always be referred to as 'that lingo'.

ON NOT KNOWING ANYTHING

ONE thing you must learn in England is that you must never really learn anything. You may hold *opinions* – as long as you are not too dogmatic about them – but it is just bad form to *know* something. You may *think* that two and two make four; you may 'rather suspect it'; but you must not go further than that. *Yes* and *no* are about the two rudest words in the language.

One evening recently I was dining with several people. Someone – a man called Trevor   suddenly paused in his remarks and asked in a reflective voice:

'Oh, I mean that large island off Africa ... You know, near Tanganyika ... What is it called?'

Our hostess replied chattily:

'I'm afraid I have no idea. No good asking me, my dear.' She looked at one of her guests: 'I think Evelyn might ... '

Evelyn was born and brought up in Tanganyika but she shook her head firmly:

'I can't remember at the moment. Perhaps Sir Robert ... '

Sir Robert was British Resident in Zanzibar – the place in question – for twenty-seven years but he, too, shook his head with grim determination:

'It escapes me too. These peculiar African names . . . I know it *is* called something or other. It may come back to me presently.'

Mr Trevor, the original enquirer, was growing irritated.

'The wretched place is quite near Dar es Salaam. It's called . . . Wait a minute . . .'

I saw the name was on the tip of his tongue. I tried to be helpful.

'Isn't it called Zan . . .'

One or two murderous glances made me shut up. I meant to put it in question form only but as that would have involved uttering the name sought for, it would not do. The word stuck in my throat. I went on in the same pensive tone:

'I mean . . . What I meant was, isn't it Czechoslovakia?'

The Vice-President of one of our geographical societies shook his head sadly.

'I don't think so . . . I can't be sure, of course . . . But I shouldn't think so.'

Mr Trevor was almost desperate.

'Just south of the equator. It sounds something like . . .'

But he could not produce the word. Then a benevolent looking elderly gentleman, with a white goatee beard smiled pleasantly at Trevor and told him in a confident, guttural voice:

'Ziss islant iss kolt Zsantsibar, yes?'

There was deadly, hostile silence in the room. Then

a retired colonel on my left leaned forward and whispered into my ear:

'Once a German always a German.'

The bishop on my right nodded grimly:

'And they're surprised if we're prejudiced against them.'

ON THE DECLINE OF MUDDLE

I HAVE always been immensely proud of English muddle and thought that in this respect we were absolute and unbeatable masters with no serious rivals. I never look at any of my books once they are published, but until recently I used to read and re-read with swelling pride a chapter on 'How to Build a Muddle' in one of my earlier works. The English idea of giving neighbouring streets almost identical names – such as Belsize Gardens, Belsize Road, Belsize Villas, Belsize Crescent, Belsize Park Road, etc., was most ingenious, likely to confuse the most cunning foreigner; and if a few of them were not confused by this, then the numbering of the houses came in: numbers running consecutively along one side of the road and back along the other; giving names to houses instead of numbers. A subtle variation is to *name* your house 'Twenty-Seven' when its number is really 359. I was also delighted to spend two years of my life as an inhabitant of Walm Lane, North-West London. I was proud of Walm Lane. Walm Lane performs the unique trick – unique even in this country – of, suddenly and unexpectedly, becoming its own side-street.

But a terrible shock awaited me. I was informed by

BELSIZE PARK GARDENS NW3
Leading to BELSIZE CRESCENT
← Nos. 1– 125 : Nos. 2–124 →
NO THROUGH ROAD TO
BELSIZE VILLAS

letter from Germany – of all places – that in a small town (I am afraid I have forgotten its name and lost the letter) they have done much, much better than we do in England. House numbers there run in chronological order: in other words, the house built first is 1, the house built next at the other end of the road is 2, then one in the middle is 3 and so on, and so on. Needless to say, the confusion achieved is consummate and the apparently daring English idea of running the numbers up one side and back down the other seems childish and amateurish in comparison.

I did not mind the loss of India. I was prepared to accept British nationality even after the Empire was gone. I even survived the loss of the Ashes. But that the Germans – the most orderly, the most tidy-minded of all peoples – should beat us at our own game and should be able to produce more senseless and more glorious muddle in their towns than we can, that, I am afraid, is the mark of our real decadence.

What next? Are we going to be thrashed at cricket by the Bulgarians? Are the Albanians going to teach us how to make Scotch whisky? Or are we – no, we cannot sink quite as low as that – are we going to introduce some sense into our weights and measures next? I am inclined to exclaim: *Après moi le déluge!* (That is a cry of despair and it means: After me the decimal system of coinage!)

HOW TO DIE

THE English are the only race in the world who enjoy dying. Most other peoples contemplate death with abject and rather contemptible fear; the English look forward to it with gusto.

They speak of death as if it were something natural. It is, of course, more natural than birth. Hundreds of millions of people are not born; but all who are born, die. During the bombing raids of the last war people on the Continent prayed: 'God, even if I have to be hit and maimed, please spare my life.' The English said: 'If I have to die, well, I couldn't care less. But I don't want to be made an invalid and I don't want to suffer.' Foreign insurance agents speak of 'certain possibilities' and the 'eventuality' that 'something might happen to you'; the English make careful calculations and the thought that the insurance company will have to pay up always sweetens their last hours. Nowhere in the world do people make so many cruel jokes about the aged and the weak as here. In Continental families you simply do not refer to the fact that a parent or a grandparent is not immortal. But not long ago my two children burst into my room and asked me:

'Daddy, which of us will get your camera when you die?'

'I'll let you know,' I replied. 'By the way, I am sorry to be still alive. It's not my fault. I can't help it.'

They were a little hurt.

'Don't be silly. We don't really mind at all. We only wanted to know who'll get the camera.'

And when the moment comes, the English make no

fuss. Dead or alive, they hate being conspicuous or saying anything unconventional. They are not a great people for famous last words.

I shall never forget the poor gentleman who once travelled with me on the Channel boat. Only the two of us were on deck as a violent storm was raging. A tremendous gale was lashing mountainous seas. We huddled there for a while, without saying anything. Suddenly a fearful gust blew him overboard. His head emerged just once from the water below me. He looked at me calmly and remarked somewhat casually:

'Rather windy, isn't it?'

ON BEING UNFAIR

BRITAIN – to its true glory – is the only country in the world where the phrase, 'it isn't fair,' still counts as an argument. The word *fair* exists in no other language and if something vaguely similar does exist, it conjures up utterly different notions. The English themselves are not quite clear as to what *fair* really means. I have two famous dictionaries in front of me – both renowned for their brief and lucid definitions – but they are rather unsatisfactory on this particular word. They say between them that, *fair* (adj.) is: of moderate quality, not bad, pretty good, favourable, promising, gentle, unobstructed, frank, honest, just, not effected by insidious or unlawful methods, not foul, civil, pleasing, honourable, etc., etc. Well fair enough. But *fair* is really something more and also much less. If something strikes the Englishman as not quite in order for one reason or another, not quite equitable, then the thing just 'isn't fair'.

Use the argument, 'this isn't fair,' to any Continental and he will gape at you without any sign of understanding. Who the hell *wants* to be fair?

On the other hand, tell an Englishman that he is stupid – and he will smile benevolently; tell him that he is obstinate, insular, selfish, cruel, uneducated, ignorant and his neck is dirty to begin with – he will shrug his shoulders. But tell him that he isn't fair and he will be pained and angered. Tell a legislator that his bill or programme will create a bloody revolution and he will be undeterred; but prove to him that it is genuinely unfair to one group or another and he will

abandon it. Or face an English assassin with a chopper in his hand and warn him that should he dare to kill you he will be hanged – he will kill you without any further ado and argument. It is only fair that a criminal should take a chance; that is in the nature of his chosen profession. But convince him that it is unfair to rob you and he will take his cap and leave. He does not greatly mind being hanged; but no English robber and murderer worthy of the name would tolerate the stigma of being unfair.

ON MINDING ONE'S OWN BUSINESS

THIS IS one of the basic English virtues. It is not to be interpreted as really minding your own business (getting on with your job, keeping your promises, etc); it simply means that you are not to interfere with others. If a man happens to be standing on your foot in the bus, you must not ask him to get off, since it is clearly his business where he chooses to stand; if your neighbour's television or radio is blaring military marches till midnight, you may not remonstrate with him because it is his business what he pleases to listen to and at what time; if you are walking peacefully in the street and someone pours two gallons of boiling water over your best bowler through his bathroom overflow, the pipe of which is aimed at the street (see: ANCIENT LIBERTIES) you should proceed without uttering a word – however short – because it is obviously the other fellow's business when he has his bath and how hot he likes it.

In the late nineteen-fifties, a man committed a

murder in the Midlands, splashing himself with blood in the process. Afterwards, near the scene of the crime a man covered with blood was seen to board a bus with about fifty people on it. Yet when he got off, leaving a pool of blood on the floor, not one single passenger bothered to ask him what he had been doing lately. They were true Britons, minding their own business.

If another man had been carrying some victim's decapitated head under his arm, that would not make the slightest difference. The parcel you carry is your own business.

I remember an old story from my childhood which ought to be one of the basic ideological parables of English life.

A man bends down in a London street to tie his shoelace. While he's at it, someone kicks him in the behind with such force that he falls on his nose. He gets up somewhat bewildered and looks at his assailant questioningly. The latter explains:

'I *am* sorry. I seem to have made a mistake. I thought you were my friend, Harry Higgins. I meant this as a joke.'

The man (presumably of foreign origin) is not altogether satisfied with this explanation and remarks plaintively:

'But even if I had been Harry Higgins . . . must you kick him quite so hard?'

The other man replies coolly and pointedly:

'What has it got to do with you *how* hard I choose to kick my friend, Harry Higgins?'

SEX

THIS seemingly most immutable of all social habits changes too – and changes fast. In an earlier volume of mine – a treatise on the English character* – I wrote a very brief chapter on this subject. It ran: 'Continental people have sex life: the English have hot-water bottles.' That was all. It has now become hopelessly out-of-date. How right was the kind (and to me unknown) lady who wrote to me in a letter:

'You are really behind the times. In this field, too, things have changed and – this is the most important – techniques have advanced. We are using electric blankets nowadays.'

And, no doubt, things will go on changing. I do not know for certain but I feel sure that A.I.D. – Artificial Insemination by Donor – was invented by Englishmen as a labour-saving device. Knowing the English character, and its marked lack of enthusiasm in this particular field, I am convinced that A.I.D. will grow immensely popular in no time and that soon it will be the rule rather than the exception.

I foresee the time – not in the too distant future, either – when a shy young man will be asked at a party:

'How are you, old man? And how's your wife? Have you A.I.D.-ed any more family lately? What's it going to be this time: a boy or a girl?'

And the bashful young man will blush and reply:

* *How to be an Alien*, by George Mikes. Nicolas Bentley drew the pictures. André Deutsch, 7s. 6d. Available at all better-class bookshops. Order *two* copies now.

'I can't be sure . . . You see, we don't A.I.D. our children. I've got a "Do It Yourself" kit.'

HOW TO AVOID WORK

MANY may wonder how the English acquired their reputation of not working as hard as most Continentals. I am able to solve this mystery. They acquired this reputation by not working as hard.

It is, by the way, all due to their lack of rhythm and nothing else. Let me explain what I mean.

In my young days there used to be a joke about a silly aristocrat – the type of hero the Austrians called Count Bobby. Count Bobby comes home from shooting and his friend, Aristide, asks him how he got on.

'Badly. I got nothing,' Bobby informs him.

'But how's that possible? It's so easy to shoot rabbits. They always run in zig-zags.'

'That's true,' Bobby nods sadly, 'but I was out of luck. Whenever I shot at zig, he was in zag; when I shot at zag, he was in zig.'

The same is true of Englishmen in general, When they work (or are in zig) they rest (zag); when they rest (zag), they work hard (zig).

On the rare occasions when two groups of Englishmen are vying with one another as to who should perform a certain job, the result is most surprising. You would naïvely assume that both groups are keen to do the job. Not at all. Whenever the Boilermakers' Union starts a quarrel with the Shipwrights' as to who should drive wooden nails into metal or metal nails into wood, they call a strike for two or three months. In other words (and this is the Basic Law of English Labour) if two Englishmen are equally eager to do a job, the job is sure to be left undone.

Normally, in the factory, workshop or office, they use their working day to build up energy for those fatiguing hours of leisure when they weed, dig and hoe the garden, play golf, redecorate the spare bedroom, build a shed in the backyard, etc., etc. It is little wonder that when at last they go to bed they are inclined to believe that the time for rest has arrived. They are in zag again all right.

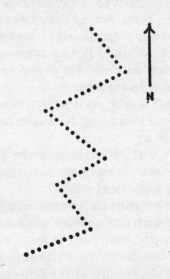

EVERYBODY IS HUNGARIAN

BUT the time has come to stop prevaricating. For the last eighty odd pages of this book – I am sorry to admit this, but it's true – I have been doing nothing but raise false hopes. You cannot become an Englishman, try as you may. Because the simple truth is this: everybody is Hungarian. This is a basic and irrefutable theorum like that of Pythagoras.

Pythagoras was no relation of mine; but I am proud to report that the second theorem was discovered by my wife. One evening, while reading a certain biography, I exclaimed: 'Oh! . . .' She looked at me enquiringly from the other armchair. I explained that I had just discovered that the parents of Alfred Adler were Hungarian. She replied briefly and concisely:

'So what?'

I do not like the expression, particularly when my important and sensational statements are greeted with it. Before I could protest, however, my wife added:

'Why shouldn't they be Hungarian? Everybody is Hungarian.'

And she returned to her book.

I do not know how Pythagoras's spouse received the news when her husband first said to her: 'I say, darling, did it ever strike you that the square on the hypotenuse, etc., etc.' But it certainly stands to my everlasting credit that as soon as my wife uttered *her* theorem I saw the light. I knew it was true and irrefutable. Of course, everybody is Hungarian. It seemed

We are all Hungarians

incredible that no one had thought of this theorem before.

It is true on various planes.

1. London is a great English city, but it is also a small Hungarian village. Most Hungarians living in London will tell you that while they do not avoid other Hungarians, it so happens that they do not know any of them. Well, of course, their immediate circle consists of Hungarians — a few former school-mates, relations, etc. — but apart from these thirty or forty people, they simply do not know any Hungarians in London. A few minutes afterwards you happen to ask them to recommend a doctor, a solicitor, a dentist, or a dressmaker and they will recommend a Hungarian doctor, solicitor, dentist, or dressmaker who is reputed to be the best in England. They happen to know a Hungarian cobbler round the corner who is a genius of his craft and a Hungarian tailor who puts Savile Row to shame. We all know where to buy Hungarian salami, sausages and apricot brandy. We all go to various Hungarian restaurants where they cook exactly as our mothers did. We go to see Hungarian dancers in Shaftesbury Avenue, to listen to Hungarian violinists in Wigmore Hall, to applaud Hungarian runners at the White City, to watch Hungarian football players at Wembley — and so on, there is always something. I do not quite know how it is with others; but I, personally, have not seen an Englishman in London for over two years.

2. Yes, of course, everybody is Hungarian. And if he isn't then his father or his grandmother was. Alexander Korda, the father of the British film industry, is one of the very obvious examples. When Leo Amery — one

of the flag-bearers of the British Imperial idea – died,
I learned from his obituaries that his mother had
been Hungarian. Leslie Howard, the incarnation, indeed the prototype – both in manners and in appearance – of the modern Briton, was . . . Well, need I go
on? I am Hungarian; André Deutsch is Hungarian.
Nicolas Bentley, by now, is at least half Hungarian.
Queen Mary was not a Hungarian. But whenever she
received a Hungarian she was fond of telling him that
two of her grandparents were.

3. You may ask: 'But what about those few –
infinitesimal as their number may be – who are, in
spite of everything, not Hungarians?'

Well, they are being Magyarized at breath-taking
speed. I know quite a few Hungarians who have not
learnt one single word of English in all the years they
have been living here. In fact, they regard it as a crying
shame and personal insult that people should talk English in this country. They go on speaking Hungarian
everywhere and to everybody and if others fail to
understand, that is their worry. The population of
London, I must say, has made remarkable progress in
the Hungarian language. There is a small café – frequented by Hungarians – where a young Yorkshire
girl greeted me the other day with '*Kezétcsókolom,
aranyas!*', which means, 'I kiss your hand, darling!'
I know of a grandmother – recently arrived from Budapest – who in the course of two years has managed to
teach her two British-born grandchildren, an Irish
maid and a Spanish governess, reasonably fluent Hungarian without herself learning a single word of
English, Irish or Spanish. The prize for good educational work, however, must go to another Hungarian

matron who was travelling on a No. 2 bus from Baker Street, meaning to get off at Platts Lane. She missed her stop, however. Reaching Cricklewood Lane and finding the surroundings unfamiliar, she jumped up, walked to the conductor – a fine and honest cockney, born and bred – and said:

'Platts Lane? *Erre?* (pointing one way) *Arra?*' (pointing the other way).

In case it is only your grandmother who was Hungarian and you yourself are not, I ought to add that *erre* means *this way,* and *arra* means *that way.*

The conductor was a little taken aback by this pantomime and asked her:

'Platts Lane, lady? If you want Platts Lane . . .'

The lady shook her head. English was not a language to which she could listen with patience. She interrupted the conductor with some irritation:

'Platts Lane? *Erre? Arra?*'

The conductor raised his voice and tried again:

'Look, lady, I'm just trying to tell you that . . .'

The lady interrupted again, this time quite peremptorily:

'Platts Lane: *erre? arra?*'

The conductor sighed and pointed backwards:

'Platts Lane? *Arra!*'

HOW TO BE AN

DECADENT

To my dear old friend, Emeric Pressburger –
the only man I know who is not decadent.
But – I hope – he can learn.

'But you are ruining the country!'

FOR SOME TIME
THERE'LL BE AN ENGLAND . . .

THESE are great years for the British. The nation has not been so gloriously united since the days of Churchill, but a blind and unappreciative world fails to see the light.

Some time ago a businessman friend of mine remarked about a Trotskyist Trade Union faction which was holding up the settlement of a damaging strike by insisting on some ludicrous and impossible demands: 'They are incredibly stupid. Don't they see that they are ruining the country?' But as their aim *was* to ruin the country they were not stupid, whatever else they may have been.

Similarly, the world fails to understand the British and appreciate what they are doing. The British – as the whole world, particularly the British themselves, keep saying – are the most fair-minded people in the world. After the Second World War they declared: 'Let's be fair. We have been Top Nation for centuries. We have done splendidly well once again. Now we must give others a chance. Let's decline.'

But it is not so easy to decline as the uninitiated imagine. After a few centuries other nations just will not believe that you are as inefficient and couldn't-careless as you are. They will insist on thinking of you as successful, reliable and rich, however unsuccessful, unreliable and poor you may have become. Declining needs the effort of a united nation – not just one class, one layer; not just the politicians. It needs the unfailing effort of rich and poor, old and young, intellectual and illiterate, skilled and unskilled, shop floor and management. It is an arduous, almost herculean task but nothing will deter the British, once they have made up their minds. They played a great part in destroying Nazi Germany; the destruction of democratic Britain seems child's play compared with that.

The general strategy was grandiose: let us give away our Empire as fast as possible or a little faster; let us ruin the pound sterling by pretending that we did not give away our Empire and can still be a reserve currency; let us ruin the City and then rely on it as our main source of strength; let us distribute overseas aid in a grand manner, at the same time, let us go around begging, cap in hand; *Made in Britain* used to be synonymous with superlative quality, so let us not rest until it means 'shoddy goods, delivered late'; and let us divide the country into small sections. If Cyprus can be independent, why not Wales? If Malta, why not Lancashire or Cornwall? If Singapore, why not Birmingham? If Field Marshal Idi Amin can make a fool of himself – well, didn't he learn everything from us?

All this needed great determination, skill and the united effort of a great nation. But the British aren't the British for nothing. To their eternal glory, they are on the way to complete success.

ON THE ELEGANCE OF DECAY

It was not only that proverbial spirit of fairness that led the nation to this decision. There was another, equally good reason. To remain Top Nation would inevitably have meant *winning* the eternal rat-race from time to time – perhaps quite often – and that the British cannot bear. The thing is to take part but not to win. You take part only and exclusively because without taking part *you cannot lose*. This is not the Nation of Vulgar Winners; this is the Nation of Good Losers.

The greatest days of Rome were its days of decline. The most splendid period of the Bourbon monarchy was the period before the Revolution. It is more elegant, wise and stylish to decay than to flourish; better to decline than to pant, rush around, sweat and get hoarse in vulgar bargaining. It is much more in keeping with the British style to live in a quiet and slightly disintegrating manor house than in a super-modern and noisy market place. It is more in keeping to potter around in the garden and remain healthy than to rush around town under great stress and get heart attacks. I agree with the British about this; I too prefer constructive decay to futile progress. But one has to *know* how to decay; one must learn how to be decadent. You may desire to decay, yet your inborn excellence, your splendid human qualities, your shining character may keep you on the top. Or else, you may overdo it and decay a shade too speedily.

* * *

Once upon a time I committed another little book, called *How to be an Alien*. A good friend, to my horror, discovered in 1976 that that book was thirty years old. I have reluctantly to admit that although I was only four years old when I wrote it, this makes me almost middle-aged.

What has changed in thirty years? *Who* has changed in thirty years? Would I write that book again? *Could* I write that book again? If I did try to write it, in what way would it differ from the original *How to be an Alien*?

Both I and Britain have, of course, changed a great deal. First of all, I have become, in a sense, more British than the British while the British have become less British. I have become a little better off than the young refugee was thirty years ago, Britain has become much poorer. I have climbed up the ladder a bit, Britain has climbed down quite a lot. I have become less of a European, Britain – apparently – more European. Britain has lost an Empire and gained me (the net gain, let's face it, is infinitesimal).

How to be an Alien was addressed to fellow aliens, telling them how to make themselves acceptable, how to imitate the English – in other, simple words *How to be an Alien* was telling them how not to be an Alien.

There was a joke at the end of the forties. A German refugee was offered naturalisation but he indignantly

Ups and downs

exclaimed: 'What? Without India?!' He had a point, of course. But should you still wish to belong to the clan – India or no India – you must go through a refresher course if you are an ancient alien like myself, or learn some new rules if you are a newcomer, a budding alien. You still have to discuss the weather, of course, with fervent interest; you still have to form an orderly queue on the slightest provocation; you are still not to address a shop-assistant until you are spoken to; if you are a worker, you are not to work, if you are a solicitor you are not to solicit, if you are a streetwalker you are not to walk the streets, if you are the Lord Privy Seal you are not a lord and if you are the Black Rod you most certainly are not black (nor, for that matter, are you a rod). But English ideas on food, drink, sex, travel etc have changed or been modified, so study the new rules carefully.

The most important thing to remain unchanged is the English attitude towards you. The world still consists of two clearly divided groups: the English and the foreigners. One group consists of less than fifty million people; the other of 3,950 million. The latter group does not really count. The Scots, the Welsh, the Irish and – more or less – the Australians and the Americans are neither English nor foreigners: they are the Scots, the Welsh, the Irish, the Australians and the Americans, but they are as ludicrous as foreigners. Bloody foreigners are rarely called bloody foreigners nowadays, some say because the English have become more polite; my own feeling is that the word 'bloody' has changed its meaning and is no longer offensive enough. You may have become a 'visitor' or even a 'distinguished European', but turn to the Oxford Dictionary and you will find (or should find, if that publication is really as accurate as it is supposed to be) that 'distinguished European' is a synonym for bloody foreigner.

It has still never occurred to one single Englishman that not everybody would regard it as a step up, as a promotion, to become English; that in the last decade or two quite a few of these bloody foreigners started regarding the English as the laughing stock of Europe and looking down upon the present generation with pity; that, indeed, many of them thank Almighty God for letting them belong to more prosperous and successful nations. No; the pound is still 'sterling', hundred mark-notes are still strange pieces of paper with some Teutonic nonsense printed on them. And if Britannia does not rule the waves, very well, that is only and exclusively because the waves and the world do not deserve it any more.

OLD AND NEW

UNDERSTATEMENT is still in the air. It is not just a speciality of the English sense of humour; it is a way of life. When gales uproot trees and sweep away roofs of houses, you should remark that it is 'a bit blowy'. I have just been listening to a man who got lost in a forest abroad for a week and was scrutinised by hungry wolves, smacking their lips. Was he terrified? – asked the television interviewer, obviously a man of Italian origin. The man replied that on the seventh day, when there were no rescuers in sight and the sixth hungry wolf joined the pack, he 'got a bit worried'. Yesterday, a man in charge of a home where six hundred old people lived, which was found to be a fire risk where all the inhabitants might burn to death, admitted: 'I may have a problem.' (Mind you: *he* may have a problem. What about the six hundred? Their's not to make reply, Their's not to reason why, Their's but to burn and die.)

* * *

Britain is still a class-ridden society. As soon as a man opens his mouth, we can tell in what sort of school he missed his education. Aliens have a tremendous advantage here: they may be beyond the pale; but they are beyond class too.

But the class system has changed. Britain has a working class which does not work; a ruling class which does not rule; and a middle class which is not in the middle but is sliding fast to the bottom.

*   *   *

Before the war you could place a man by his clothes. The rich – particularly at weekends – went around in rags; the working class wore cloth caps; prostitutes wore foxes round their necks and smoked cigarettes in the street; wives of rich brewers wore mink coats and wives of dustmen were dressed as today only Eliza Doolittle is in revivals of *My Fair Lady*. Today mink has become vulgar and the Marks and Spencer era has abolished class differences in dress. There are tricks, of course, and there is Dior, of course, but by simply looking at a woman you can no longer tell whether her husband is a struggling property developer or a rich dustman.

Not long ago my blue raincoat was taken away in the Garrick Club by mistake by one of our noble lords – keys in the pocket and all – and I was left with the other man's blue raincoat – keys in the pocket and all. The noble lord wrote me a letter of apology: 'My only excuse is that a Marks and Spencer raincoat resembles a John Collier raincoat to such an extent. . . .'

*   *   *

Before the war people came here to settle only when they were driven to do so: refugees and immigrants. (In

The cloth-cap image

those days immigrants could be white. But we were white Negroes, really. Today a Negro, as a rule, is black, except that no black man may be called a Negro.) No one settled in this country who was not forced to. Today, fellow-aliens from happy and prosperous countries flock here: Germans, Americans, Swedes, Arabs and many others. The British are poor – slightly beggarly, even – but well-mannered, good-humoured, tolerant and civilised. Their elegant decadence is the magnet that draws people here. The English, on the other hand, leave in large numbers. Their exodus is called the brain drain and includes a fair number of the completely brainless, too. The emigrés are old-fashioned Imperialists who want cash and security. Similar exchanges of population occurred after the war in the Sudeten regions of Czechoslovakia or the former German regions of today's Poland, for example – but those exchanges were enforced, these are voluntary. England will soon be full of completely anglicised immigrants from California, Frankfurt, Port of Spain and Jeddah while other lands will be full of frustrated and morose Britons. Mr Enoch Powell is barking up the wrong tree. If he wants to live among white Englishmen, all he has to do is move to Kuwait.

LANGUAGE

In my early days there were stories about funny refugees murdering the English language. A refugee woman goes to the greengrocer to buy red oranges (I mean red inside), very popular on the Continent and called blood oranges.

'I want two pounds of bloody oranges.'

'What sort of oranges, dear?' asked the greengrocer, a little puzzled.

'Bloody oranges.'

'Hm . . .' He thinks. 'I see. For juice?'

'Yes, we are.'

Another story dates from two years later. By that time the paterfamilias – the orange-buying lady's husband – has become terribly, terribly English. He meets an old friend in Regents Park, and instead of talking to him in good German, softly, he greets him in English, loudly.

'Hallo, Weinstock. . . . Lovely day, isn't it? Spring in the air.'

'Why should I?'

And on one occasion I received a written message from an Austrian gentleman, that he wanted to speak to me urgently 'in the nearest convenience'.

Those days are over. Not only former refugees but the

whole world has learnt to speak proper English. Pronunciation is another matter; the refugee may still be the man who has lost everything except his accent. On the other hand, Central European has become one of the legitimate accents of English. Or the trouble with the foreign student may be that his English is too good, too precise, too correct. 'He speaks English too well, he must be a bloody foreigner,' is a frequent comment. And a just one, too, because while the rest of the world is busy learning English, the English themselves are busy forgetting their beautiful mother-tongue. If you want to sound a proper Englishman use no more than eight hundred words and, preferably, about half of them incorrectly. Most Englishmen will tell you that 'English has no grammar', which is just another way of saying that *they* have no grammar. Not long ago I kept seeing Post Office vans with the attractive slogan: 'Everyone should have a phone of their own.' In a letter to the *Guardian* I remarked: 'But I think nearly everyone do already.' A number of correspondents wrote in to tell me off as a pedant and a prig, remarking that the Post Office had used good 'colloquial' English.

Before the war a spade used to be a spade – often brutally so. I remember an institution named *Hospital for Incurable Diseases*. How gentle, how tactful, I thought and tried to imagine the feelings of the patient driven through the gates. But by today a dustman has become a refuse collector, a policeman a law enforcement officer, the pilot of a plane a captain, a man who sells second-hand socks from a market stall a business executive and a dog a home-protection officer.

If you want to sound truly English, you must learn to

speak the language really badly. It will not be difficult, there are many language schools where they teach you exactly that. (If you are unlucky you may choose one of the old-fashioned ones and be taught English as it should be, and not as it is, spoken.) Remember that everything is a 'situation' or a 'problem' nowadays. In the old days a man was travelling, today he is in a travel situation. In the past he got married, today he finds himself in a marriage situation. In the past he went bankrupt, today he has a liquidity problem. In the old days he was impotent, today he has a virility problem.

In our economic plight rationing has already begun. This is kept a secret and for the time being only the letter *r* is rationed. The modern Englishman has a certain number of *r*-s at his disposal and no more. He – and that applies even to some radio announcers – uses them foolishly. He will speak of *Indiar-and-Pakistan* and of *Lawr-and-order*, only to find that he used up his *r*-ration, frittered it away, and now he has to save madly where he can. So he will speak of a Labouh M.P. and of the Fah East.

Do we really have a serious *r*-problem? Or are we just in an illiteracy situation?

FOOD

'On the Continent people have good food; in England they have good table manners,' I wrote in *How to be an Alien*. Since then, food in England has improved, table manners have deteriorated. In those days food was hardly ever discussed, it was taboo, like sex. Today newspapers and magazines all have their good food guides and many so-called experts send you off to eat uneatable meals. Then it was possible for a much-travelled businessman, even a diplomat, to have no idea what an avacado pear was; today any docker may quarrel with his wife: 'What's that Doris, paëlla? Paëlla again? All right, I know I like paëlla but paëlla *every* day – bloody paëlla and nothing else? What about a decent, honest-to-goodness ratatouille for a change?'

There is no denying that the post-war travelling mania has improved British eating habits beyond recognition. Before the war, the French loved eating and were proud of it; the puritanical British loved eating just as much but were ashamed of their passion. After the war, millions of people got acquainted with good food abroad and refused the staple diet of stale boiled cabbage floating in tepid, salt water. You could eat very well in London in the sixties and seventies. Even Michelin published a guide to British restaurants, partly to pay tribute to this improvement, partly to emphasise that in spite of all improvements not one single British establishment deserved three rosettes.

That much-boasted improvement, however, is not quite so universal as we should like to believe. In 1976 the police noticed that a large number of foreign lorry-drivers were committing speeding offences. They were driving their enormous articulated lorries as if they were racing cars or as if they were being pursued. Investigation established that they were, in fact, pursued: by English food. They were doing their level best – risking their licences and even their lives – to get away from English meals. They wanted to deliver their goods and return to the Continent on the same day. As they had to eat *something* while in Britain, most of them – according to the UICR, the Union Internationale des Chauffeurs Routiers – brought decent continental sandwiches with them.

There is another remarkable development. In those early days one could not find one single English restaurant on the Continent and very few in London. Soho was full of Italian, Greek, Chinese, Spanish and Hungarian restaurants. Yugoslav and Portuguese places came later, to be joined before long by beefburger and Kentucky fried chicken establishments, Wimpy bars and other glories of American civilisation; but proper English restaurants were few and far between even in London. Today, almost everything that is bad in the English kitchen is becoming popular on the Continent while everything that is good is going out of fashion even in Britain.

Take the English breakfast, for example, the true glory of English culinary art which puts the pale and insipid *café complet* to shame. Is it gaining ground in Oslo or Luxembourg? On the contrary – and it has almost completely disappeared from English homes and is fast disappearing even from English hotels. You can make your own breakfast in some hotels from instant coffee or tea supplied in little bags, or you may be served scrambled eggs made of top-quality plastic mixed with outstandingly tasty cotton wool.

But other things English are gaining ground. Fish and chip shops (this is an exception to the rule: fish and chips is one of the glories of Britain) are being opened all over Europe and British cod is being wrapped in the *Daily Mirror* – after all, you cannot wrap up fish and chips in the *Dagens Nyheter* and still less in the *Frankfurter Allgemeine Zeitung*. So far so good. Fish and chip shops are great institutions, but the true horrors and monstrosities of the English kitchen are becoming even more popular.

English grocer-shops are being opened in Brussels and other places where true Britons congregate in large numbers. They sell canned steak and kidney pud, English sausages, porridge, cans of oxtail and mulligatawny soups, baked beans, tomato ketchup and other outrages on the human palate. You might have thought that the British leave this country in order to get away from all this. Not at all. They queue up for them all over Europe. I am happy to report that these imports have not made any impact yet on the Continentals. As soon as the French start queuing up for baked beans, I shall commit harakiri, simply by leaning slowly on my

'Watch it, mate, I ain't eatin' my chips out o' some bloody foreign paper.'

favourite carving knife. Yes: the day the French start eating canned steak and kidney pie with a little tomato ketchup on top will mark the end of a great civilisation, the end of European supremacy and the suicide of a Continent.

*　　*　　*

And a final warning to continental visitors. Many have come to grief, not knowing an important British custom.

At dinner parties – on the Continent as well as in Britain – you will be offered a second helping. On the Continent – particularly in Austria but also in other Central European lands – you say 'No thank you' upon which the hostess will shriek, moan, sob and beseech you to eat a little more. She will accuse you of not liking her food, of spoiling her evening, of making her unhappy, of being unappreciative and ungrateful, a bad guest and a bad man. So you protest your appreciation, assure her that the food is magnificent, one of the memorable meals of your life, take a lot more of everything, force it down, get indigestion, and speed on to an early demise.

All Continentals, brought up in Mönchengladbach, Attnang-Pucheim, Hódmezövásárhely or Subotica, start off in Britain, too, with an innocent 'No thank you' as their mothers taught them. And that is the end of the affair. To their horror, the hostess does not fall on her knees and does not threaten suicide if her guest does not make a pig of himself. With rueful eyes the poor guest sees the dishes disappear, and the subject is closed.

So when offered a second helping, grab it. Or simply

nod. No one will think the worse of you. And no one will regard you as a gentleman for not taking a second helping. No one will regard you as a gentleman whatever you may do – so you might as well take that second helping.

DRINKS

DRINKS have gone in or out of fashion, like clothes. When I first came here, gin and lime was the most popular drink. Ask for a gin and lime today and people will look at you as if thinking you must have fought with the Duke of Wellington's army. Then came the pink gin era. Apart from a few fossils, who drinks pink gin today? Whisky, of course, has remained a favourite and vodka has become popular. (Justly so. Vodka today is 2.7 per cent stronger than in Czarist times. Some sceptics doubt that this one single achievement of the Soviet State justifies sixty years of upheaval, misery, Stalin, purges and the Gulag Archipelago – where, by the way, not much vodka is consumed by the prisoners.)

During the post-war years the English have learnt a great deal about wine and Britain is now *par excellence*, the land of wine snobbery, beaten only by the United States. The British love sweet wine but all deny this with a vehemence worthy of a better cause because they know (or believe) that drinking sweet wine is non-U. Excellent and expensive dry continental wines are being shipped here, then a little glucose is added to them, in secret. As a French wine expert once remarked to me: 'The English like their wine dry as long as it's sweet.'

British drinking habits are also gaining ground abroad. Whisky, and gin and tonic, have long been favourites among knowledgeable Continentals but nowadays British-style pubs are being opened all over Europe and ale is on draft at many places. Serious Belgians – Flemings and Walloons alike – sip Guinness and nod approval. But if the expansion of British ale is a little surprising, the conquering march – well, the few conquering steps – of British wine is downright flabbergasting.

More and more people maintain that Britain is a vine-growing country. If it could be done under Elizabeth I why not under Elizabeth II? What's wrong with *our* Elizabeth? A friend of mine, in a high and responsible job and otherwise quite normal, keeps reassuring me in all seriousness that his own wine, grown in Fulham, beats any French and German wine hands down. As he produces only twenty-eight bottles per annum of his *Château Parsons Green*, Pouilly Fumé and Niersteiner need not tremble yet. But they'd better watch Fulham. I tried his wine in Chelsea, in a house some five hundred yards from the Fulham border. It was vinegary, indeed undrinkable, and we were all embarrassed – except for him. 'I admit,' he said generously, 'that fine though this wine is, it doesn't travel very well.'

In the mid-sixties I wrote a book on snobbery with the Duke of Bedford. Once, after dinner, I asked him what his own, worst snobbery was.

'What exactly do you mean?' he asked.

'Something you know is snobbish and silly, still you stick to it.'

He did not have to think long: 'I'd rather bite my tongue off than say "cheers".'

'What *do* you say? Skål?'

'Nothing, of course. That's the point. A man likes to drink in peace and does not want attention drawn to himself whenever he lifts his glass to his lips. Just drink and keep silent.'

For a while this rule was followed in U circles. But today people do not want to be U any more. Besides, the one strong measure the Chancellor has taken to solve the economic crisis, is to raise the price of drinks higher and higher. That is supposed to save the country. Like taking in one another's washing. So the drinkers of Britain are really saving us all. Drinking another double whisky is an act of patriotism. Even pink gin. And vodka, too. England expects every man to do his duty.

SHOPPING

WHEN you, Distinguished Visitor, want to do some shopping in England, you are – as you will find out soon – at the mercy of the shop-assistants, now called sales ladies or sales gentlemen, soon to be called Knights and Dames of the Barter. Shopping here is different from shopping elsewhere.

1. When you enter the shop, as likely as not, the Knights and Dames of the Barter will be engaged in lively and witty conversation with one another. You must wait until they turn their attention to you and that may take quite a while. Under no circumstances are you to interrupt their conversation; you are not to speak until you are spoken to.

2. If there are other people waiting in the shop – be the shop the local butcher's where you intend to buy a quarter of a pound of minced meat or Cartier's, where you mean to spend a quarter of a million on a ring for your girl-friend – you wait for your turn. If the death ·enalty is ever to be restored in Britain, it will not be for murder – an art the English admire and appreciate as connoisseurs – but for queue-jumping, the most heinous ·f all crimes.

3. While – say – the butcher serves a lady who is

'You are my heart's delight!'

shopping for five days for her family of fourteen, you must not take advantage of a momentary pause (as you would in France) to butt in and ask if he has any calf's liver – not because you want to be served out of turn, of course, just to find out whether it is worth waiting. You will get no reply. This is not discourtesy : it is simply due to the fact that you do not exist. You may not be aware of this; you may live in the mistaken belief that you do exist, but you do not. Before your turn comes you are less than a dog. A dog would be noticed and urged to leave the shop. But you definitely do not exist before your turn comes, you are a non-person, you are thin air, a nonentity, a body non-incarnate, waiting to be material- ised when the butcher turns his smiling attention to you.

4. Few British people go shopping because they need something, still less because they can afford it. Shopping is a social occasion – an opportunity for a chat, an oppor- tunity to display your charm, to show the world that you are on Christian-name terms with the butcher's second assistant and not just a casual who has dropped in from the street. When your turn comes, the butcher's full attention will be yours. No one exists but you. You are the centre of his universe and that's quite something. You may wax a trifle impatient when – having already waited fifty-seven minutes in the queue, ankle-deep in sawdust – the lady with the large family starts explain- ing to the butcher which of her children loves liver and which prefers kidney, or when she enquires if the butcher's younger daughter has already had her second baby. You should suppress this impatience. When your turn comes, the butcher will be yours and only yours. *You* can then discuss with him last night's rain, your

digestion, your children's progress in arithmetic, the topless lady's photo in today's *Sun* (but not politics or indeed anything that a reasonably intelligent adult would like to discuss with his favourite butcher). In France they would interrupt you with some rude remark; in Italy they would howl and burst out in ribald laughter; in Greece they would set fire to the shop. But you are in England, among tolerant and understanding Britons who are waiting patiently not so much for their meat as for their turn to chat with the butcher.

5. On entering or leaving the shop you do not greet the shopkeeper. Your first words should be: 'Have you got . . .' or 'May I have . . .' your last: 'Thank you'. In between, as explained, you may discuss any subject from the shopkeeper's grandchildren to Arsenal's chances against Liverpool, but never say 'Goodbye' or 'Hallo', or 'Cheerio', or 'Grüss Gott' or 'Ciao'.

SEX

I HAVE never been so much abused for anything I have written as for the shortest chapter I have ever produced in my life, a chapter on the sex-life of the English. People kept pointing out to me that the English multiply somehow and survive as a nation. This, surprisingly, is true.

Nowadays they also point out that London is – or was, for a time – the sex capital of the world. Let them believe it, it makes them happy.

The sex-life of the English is in strange contradiction with their placid temperament. In everything else (e.g. queueing, driving) they are reserved, tolerant and disciplined; in their sex life they tend to be violent and crude. A surprisingly large number of Englishmen like to be flogged by ladies wearing black stockings and nothing else; they believe that those ubiquitous places where women strip and show themselves stark naked to an audience, for a modest fee, are evidence of virility; they think that the high circulation of porn magazines is a sign of high sexuality and not of high neurosis. They fail to see why sweating, topless waitresses should put you off food *and* sex at one and the same time.

They also fail to see that a beautiful woman's knee in

'*Again, again, my enchantress!*'

elegant stockings is more alluring and exciting than the sight of a naked sexual organ. They are misled by their noble democratic principles which proclaim that justice must not only be done but must be seen to be done. They think that it applies to the female organ, too. It must not only be there; it must be seen to be there.

People have asked me many times – with an ironical glint in their eyes – if I still believed (as I wrote in 1946) that 'Continental people have sex-life; the English have hot-water bottles.' Or do I agree that things have changed and progressed? Yes, I agree, things *have* progressed. Not on the Continent, where people still have sex-lives; but they have progressed here because the English now have electric blankets. It is a pity that electricity so often fails in this country.

The fact remains that England may be a copulating country but it is not an erotic country. Whenever I try to personify sex in England, Lord Longford or Mrs Whitehouse spring to mind. Girls are being taken to bed, to be sure, but they are not courted; they are being made love to but they are not pursued. Women are quite willing to go to bed but they rarely flirt with men. Ladies between the ages of eight and eighty (let's say eighty-five) come back from Italy outraged and complaining bitterly about the crude wolf-whistles. Crude they may be, but they do make middle-aged ladies feel twenty-five years younger, wanted and desired, and these complaints are just disguised boasts. When bishops, retired brigadiers or at least young executives start wolf-whistling in this town of ours, then I may believe that London has become – well, not the sex capital of the world – but a budding sex-village.

Another thing that has changed in the last decades is the position of homosexuals. It is a far cry from the inhuman persecution of Oscar Wilde to public demonstrations that homosexual marriages should be legalised. (I have heard of a grafitto at an American University which claimed: 'Legalise necrophilia!' But this is not a popular movement here, as yet.)

I have only one serious objection against homosexuals. They are the most humourless bunch of people on earth – as homosexuals. As individuals, I am sure, they must be like the rest of us: some endowed with an exquisite sense of humour, others crushing bores. But as a group it is a different story. The persecution of the Jews generated some of the funniest, most self-critical and self-deprecatory yet cleverest jokes on earth; persecution of homosexuals has created jokes only against them, never by them. In fact, today you may tell jokes about Jews, black people, Scots, the Irish, dentists, policemen, dictators, our own politicians and even cats; you may tell drinking jokes, jokes about adultery and shaggy-dog stories. In other words you may joke about anything you choose except homosexuals. That is the one sacred cow, the one taboo. Should you break that taboo, however innocent your joke, any homosexual present will attack you with flashing eyes for being a reactionary fossil, an insensitive twerp and an enemy of progress. I wouldn't even mind that. They are humourless – so what? That is their business. But why on earth don't they call themselves gloomy, lugubrious, dejected, glum, mopish, sullen or grim? Why *gay*, the one thing they are not?

ON CAT-WORSHIP

HAVING joked for decades about how the English worship the cat, like the ancient Egyptians only more so, I have fallen for the cat myself. It has become *my* sacred animal.

It all started with a little black cat visiting me. 'I like it here,' she declared, and kept turning up. I thought it would be courteous to call her by a name when talking to her but I had no idea what her name was. I had to call her by the generic name of *Cica*, the Hungarian for *pussy*. (Later, she started spelling her name Tsi-Tsa because she spells everything phonetically.) I felt embarrassed at not being able to offer her anything to eat, just as one feels the need to offer a cup of coffee or a drink even to casual visitors, so I started buying cat-food. I did not know then what I know now; that this is the way of stealing somebody else's cat.

One day I was caught red-handed. In a little supermarket I had a tin of cat-food in my hand when a nice-looking blonde lady came up to me, threw a glance at the object in my hand and asked me somewhat pointedly if I was the gentleman who lived in that little red-brick house round the corner. I admitted I was he. 'My cat keeps visiting you,' she said firmly. 'I know,' I replied.

'I started feeding her not realising that I was not supposed to do so. Too late now. She expects to be fed.'
'That's all right,' said the kind lady. 'We can share her
from now on.' She added: 'This would have been a
tragedy two years ago. I have a son who just adored that
cat. But he is fourteen now and he has reached an age
when he is more interested in girls than in cats.' 'That's
perfect timing,' I told her, 'because I have reached an age
when I'm getting more interested in cats than in girls.'

So we shared Tsi-Tsa. That's how I got hold of half a
cat. Friends started guessing which half of her belonged
to me. The *Tsi* or the *Tsa*? There were some ribald sug-
gestions that it was the *Tsa*. Then difficulties arose in her
original home: a new tenant on the ground floor kept
locking the door against her and she could not get in
and out. She got fed up with that and moved over to me
completely.

By this time I was a great admirer of her sovereign
views, her incorruptibility, her coolness to human
flattery; her aloofness; her arrogance; her playfulness
(when *she* wanted to play); her affectionate nature (when
she needed affection). Some people asked me why I kept
a cat. But I did not keep a cat. It never occurred to me to
keep a cat. She has chosen me and moved in. You can
keep a dog; but it is the cat who keeps people because
cats find humans useful domestic animals.

A dog will flatter you but you have to flatter a cat. A
dog is an employee; the cat is a free-lance.

I was hurt when some cat-lovers started making
derogatory remarks: 'You have only *one* cat?' they
asked. Then Ginger turned up. I had to call him Ginger
because once again I did not know his name. He claimed

to be terribly hungry, so I had to feed him. It turned out eventually that he was no stray, he belonged to a lady next door, he has a good home but a voracious appetite. So he turns up for his breakfast every morning and knocks on my door with his paw when he arrives. As Tsi-Tsa is madly jealous, Ginger is fed in the patio. He is generous and sometimes he arranges breakfast-parties for other cats. Always the same two cats are invited and they eat together in a pleasant and friendly manner. It is all rather formal. I was told by neighbours – who know all the cats in the neighbourhood – that one of the guests is actually Ginger's son, the other his sister-in-law.

Other cats know about these feasts. They keep turning up and looking at me with an air of expectancy. I resist becoming the useful domestic animal of more and more cats but I know I am fighting a losing battle. The stray cats of Fulham have got my name and address.

Some friends believe that I am overdoing things with Tsi-Tsa. Not quite so much as Dezsö Szomory, a brilliant but eccentric and misanthropic Hungarian writer of an earlier generation. He hated human beings but loved and respected his cat. He promised an article for Christmas to a newspaper but failed to deliver it on time. A frantic editor rang him up several times. In the end he put a sheet of paper on his desk but before he could start writing his cat lay down on the paper, as cats are wont to do. To move the cat was out of the question but the article was really urgent by now. So he wrote the article *around the cat*. (The manuscript, I am told, is still preserved in Budapest.)

I have not done that as yet but I see the point. Whenever Tsi-Tsa sits on my chair – at the desk or at the table

'May I introduce my sister-in-law?'

when I want to eat – I move her chair gently and get another chair for myself. I have been late for appointments, failed to go shopping and missed planes because Tsi-Tsa was sitting on my lap. 'But why don't you throw her down?', quite a few astonished people have asked me. But I am equally astonished by such questions. You don't throw a fellow being down. You don't treat her that way just because she happens to be a cat. That would be real racial discrimination: the human race discriminating against the feline race.

ON HOW NOT TO BE RESERVED

'THE trouble with the English,' a Cypriot restaurant owner in Islington told me, 'is that they are not reserved enough.'

'You mean that they are much too reserved,' I corrected him.

'That's what I thought for a long time, too. I concentrated all my energies on making them less reserved, less stiff. On making them relaxed; at least on one single occasion; at least in my own restaurant.'

'But you never succeeded,' said I.

'Alas, I did. On New Year's Eve this restaurant was chock full, I had to send clients away. The atmosphere, the ambiance was marvellous. People started talking to one another across the tables, even flirting with one another. At midnight glasses were raised, strange people drank champagne together, they embraced and kissed. They sang Auld Lang Syne in chorus and started dancing – everybody in the restaurant, not a single soul stayed at the tables. I never thought this was possible in this country. I was really happy. And even that was not all. They marched round and round the tables, then it became much too hot and someone had the bright idea of leading the lot of them out and they danced round and round the square. I have never seen a happier and more hilarious crowd even in Nicosia than those dancers in the square.'

'Then what are you complaining about?'

'Only half of them came back.'

ON THE NATIONAL PASSION

QUITE a few people told me that I was mistaken when I made fun of the English queueing habit. It was simply a war-time expediency, it was explained to me, and it would disappear in no time.

It is still with us and will remain with us forever because it corresponds to an inner need, it is a way of self-expression. Other nations need occasional outbursts of madness and violence; the English need occasional excesses of self-discipline. Other nations, under unbearable stress, shout, howl, get into brawls, run amok; the English queue up for a cup of tea.

Demonstrations in other countries are violent affairs, with baton charges and mass arrests. Such things have occurred here, too, in the past. Today, if you are bored, you arrange a demo. It may be about the fraternal visit of some objectionable eastern potentate, or it may just as likely be a protest against the late delivery of the morning mail, or the exclusion of dachshunds from comprehensive education. It may be a demo by coloured citizens because too few of their relatives are allowed in to the country, or a demo by Enoch Powell's supporters against letting in too many. It may be a demo by bread delivery men against the low price of bread or by housewives against the high price of bread. Whether it is a demo by stamp-collectors for more special issues or by pacifists for the abolition of nuclear weapons, it does not matter, the picture will always be the same: a peaceful, smiling crowd marching, carrying boards with slogans and accompanied by a large number of bored policemen. All they will achieve is a gigantic traffic jam but that's better than nothing. Indeed, judging by some demonstrators' looks at frustrated motorists, it must be quite satisfactory.

In shops the English stand in queues; in government offices they sit in queues; in churches they kneel in queues; at sales time, they lie in queues all night in Oxford Street.

I was queueing myself once at the snack-bar of Hurlingham Club. The queue was long. In front of me there was a patient and silent middle-aged English couple and in front of them three crazy foreign women talking to one another in loud voices and with atrocious German accents. They had forgotten to collect their cutlery when joining the queue and they had forgotten to collect their salad from a side-table, so they were rushing backward and forward, cackling 'I am *so* sorry' with what they must have believed to be impeccable English manners. When they broke the sacred order of the queue once again, the taciturn Englishman started losing his temper and was obviously about to say something rather strong, when his wife warned him: 'Don't, Giles, they're not English.'

That settled it. The man calmed down and took no further notice of the three irritating females. As they were not English one could not expect them to behave.

'Ssh – I think she's probably foreign.'

Perhaps one *could* train hedgehogs, chimpanzees or foreigners to queue up in an orderly fashion, but it is not worth the trouble.

Yes, I do see the tormenting need in the English for frequent bouts of self-discipline. So I used to be puzzled by the behaviour of football fans. How did their nauseating vandalism fit my theory? I had to investigate, and my findings are not at all surprising: 97.2 per cent of all supporters of Manchester United are foreigners, mostly Dutch and Albanians. Of the rest, 2.8 per cent are Irish and Czechoslovakian, which leaves just a handful of English supporters. After the defeats of their Club these two or three English people queue up for cigarettes, then for sandwiches, then for beer, and having let off steam in true English fashion, they go home to queue up for their supper. The rest? No, Giles, they are not English.

ON NOT COMPLAINING

You must never complain. Complaining is very un-English. If you are kept waiting half an hour in a shop by the Knights of the Barter; if a bus conductor or a Labour Exchange official is rude to you; if a waiter brings your food ice-cold – you keep your mouth shut. Sometimes in a shop, in offices or some other public place an offensive or sarcastic remark may be made about you in the third person, but you just don't hear it. The stiff upper lip is the British way. Only the Dutch and the Albanians (with a few odd Irish, Czechoslovaks and suchlike thrown in) will make a row, protest loudly or call for the manager.

Should you be so misguided as to complain, or at least murmur, public opinion will instantly turn against you: 'Who does he think he is?'

The waiter may pour tomato juice down your collar and you exclaim 'Ouch!' Someone will be sure to remark: 'It's difficult to please some people.'

So do not complain. Never complain. Whatever happens, remember the new national slogan: *It's one of those things.* When your brand-new toasting machine goes up in flames and toasts you instead of your bread, you nod: 'It's one of those things,' and the matter is closed. Apart from being utterly un-English, un-Scottish and un-Welsh to complain, there is another reason for not opening your mouth. They do not even hear the complaints; their ears are not tuned to them.

A friend of mine, a film writer, was a regular client at a famous and expensive Soho restaurant. At 2 p.m. precisely (and at 9 p.m. at dinner time), the office door opened and an elderly gentleman in morning coat came out (as he had been doing for the last thirty-seven years), went from table to table, bowed slightly and asked: 'Did you enjoy your meal?' For thirty-seven years hundreds of thousands of properly brought up English people replied to him: 'Very much indeed.' The man bowed once again, said 'Thank you very much,' and moved on to the next table.

One day the lunch was so abominable that my friend (Dutch mother, Albanian father, one Irish, one Czecho-slovakian grandmother) decided to tell him the naked truth. At 2 o'clock the door opened and the antiquated manager came out as usual. When he reached my friend's table he bowed and asked yet again the question he had asked a million times in thirty-seven years 'Did you enjoy your meal, sir?'

My friend replied: 'Not at all. It was lousy.'

The manager bowed with his customary, obsequious smile: 'Thank you very much, sir.'

And moved on, satisfied.

BANK HOLIDAYS

It is the sign of a poor society that it has too many holidays. A poor society is often a religious society: it has given up all hope that the government will improve its lot so it puts its hope in God. England used to have five holidays per annum and that was that. Then she added New Year's Day because of the prevailing 'absenteeism' on that day: nobody worked in any case. Soon there was talk in some places of making Wednesday afternoons holidays, too: everyone slipped away to watch football matches, so nobody worked in any case. Then England started messing about with substitute, supplementary and compensatory holidays. When Christmas Day and Boxing Day fell on Saturday and Sunday, the Government decided that the following Monday was Christmas Day and Tuesday Boxing Day. (Jesus was not born on December 25 in any case; and what has modern Christmas to do with Jesus?) When New Year's Day fell on a Saturday (as in 1977), Monday January 3 became a holiday, because what will the poor worker gain from being an absentee, whether official or not, on a day when he would have been absent anyway? There'd be no fun in it. In 1976-77 Christmas plus New Year lasted for two weeks, and this is only the dawn of the shape of things to come.

The world looks at Britain askance. Why don't they work? Why don't they, at least, pretend to work? The world, as usual, does not understand. We, the noble British, have three excellent reasons for acting as we do: because we are 1, realists; 2, moral; and 3, practical.

1. As we are a poor nation we behave like a poor nation. We are neither snobbish (not in that way) nor pretentious – so why act like a rich nation? Other poor nations have a lot of holidays, so we shall have lots and lots of holidays. We shall stop work as often as possible and become poorer still. We must be modest and give the Germans and other industrious blokes the chance of working hard, becoming richer and making the money we want to borrow from them.

2. We are moral. We hate absenteeism and the lies it involves. One way of curing theft is to make it legal. One way of decreasing the number of violent sexual crimes is to permit rape. One way of disposing of the nasty, dishonest habit of absenteeism is to let employees off altogether.

3. The final reason is purely practical and based on sound economic assessment. Whether we work or not makes hardly any difference. So it is only sensible to save electricity, coal, administration, fares and effort.

Celebration of the birth of Christ

BUSES

Bus drivers still play the happy games described in *How to be an Alien* (available in all the better bookshops). But the buses have become much more sociable than they used to be.

Nowadays they travel in groups of three. You have to wait forty or fifty minutes for a bus, but then you get three at a time, so you are amply compensated. It always makes me feel happy and prosperous whenever I travel in three buses at one and the same time.

Bus crews, on the other hand, explain that they *must* travel in groups of three, to protect themselves against the wrath and lynching mood of the public. 'But why should the public be so angry?' – I asked. 'Because we always travel in groups of three.'

HOW TO GET LOST IN LONDON

MEASURES to confuse the foreigner and drive him to despair have developed greatly in the last thirty years, largely in the shape of new one-way streets and forbidden turnings either to the left or right. There are parts of London which even the native no longer tries to approach by car. But these methods are employed with much ingenuity in other countries as well, so I will confine this chapter to the results of my continuing research into the long-established and specifically English tricks which I first touched on thirty years ago.

1. Some streets, like Walm Lane in Cricklewood or Farm Lane in Fulham, take a ninety-degree turn and thus become their own side streets. If you continue straight along Walm Lane (coming from Shoot Up Hill) you will in fact be in another street; in order to stay in Walm Lane you have to turn sharp left.

2. As a number of cunning foreigners were learning how to find their way about in spite of all the hazards, the authorities stepped in by failing to put up – or perhaps by taking down – many signs which might have given away necessary information. Side streets, as a rule, are still indicated: their names are displayed somewhere near the corner, if not actually on it, and all you need

remember is that the name-plate is likely to be positioned higher up or lower down than you would expect which adds piquancy to the search if you are driving and the traffic is moving fast. But to find the name of a main thoroughfare is often well-nigh impossible. The official explanation is that everybody *knows* the main roads so why waste money on signs? A brilliant argument. Show me, after all, the man from Melton Mowbray, Amsterdam, or Bloomington (Illinois) who doesn't recognise at first sight any section of the Seven Sisters Road.

3. Private citizens help in their modest way by keeping house numbers secret. They refrain from putting numbers on their gates or front doors, they do not light numbers up, and – cleverest of all – they give names to their houses instead of numbers. The Dutch guilder may be temporarily stronger than the pound, but what Dutchman would have the flair to guess that 'Fairy Orchard' is to be found between numbers 117 and 121 on a street seven miles long?

But I have to admit that my chauvinism has been badly shaken by a letter from a girl who lives in a German village. She had read the relevant chapter in my earlier book and she was frankly disdainful of our methods. Her village, she said, beats London hands down – and it does. They have had the brilliant idea of numbering their houses in *chronological order*. The first house to be built is therefore Number 1, although it stands halfway along the main street. The second to be built, which stands at the beginning of the street at the eastern end, is Number 2. Number 3, the third to be built, is on the opposite side and at the western end, and so on. I have long been prepared to grant that the Germans are more methodical and systematic than we are, but to find that they can beat us in creating muddle – that hurts. At that I have to cry: Halt! Britannia, awake! Decadence *can* go too far.

HOW TO PANIC QUIETLY

FOREIGN newspapers and magazines never stop sending correspondents here to investigate the 'English disease', to analyse our decline and our despair and panic as we cower in the economic gutter. They arrive here to find no panic, no despair. With their logical minds they know that they ought to find them; but they don't. When they discuss the matter with the British, they expect some defence of this lackadaisical attitude, or excuses for certain failures. But what the British say is this: 'Yes, I quite agree, aren't we in an awful mess?' 'Oh, we are hopeless,' they say and order another double whisky. Try to discuss the pound tactfully, and they reply jovially, almost proudly: 'Yes, I wonder how anything can sink so low,' and they ring up their travel agent to book a skiing holiday in Switzerland. The foreign observer expects the British nation to sink into deep despondency whenever the pound falls two cents and be overjoyed when it gains half a cent. But most Britons have no idea – except on the days of greatest crisis – whether the pound has risen or fallen, and the nation is as calm as it was in 1940 when Hitler was about to cross the Channel but didn't.

One day you may confront one of these foreign journalists, so I should like to draw attention to a few of their stock questions and offer you the proper, British answers.

Q. Why don't the British panic?

A. They do, but very quietly. It is impossible for the naked eye to tell their panic from their ecstasy.

Q. Why don't they work harder?

A. They just don't like hard work. The Germans have a reputation for hard work, so they like to keep it up. The British find it boring. Then, apart from a tiny and despicable minority, the British dislike the idea of taking part in the rat race. They will give up certain advantages – knowingly and with their eyes open – in order to be able to stick to certain values and a way of life.

Q. But do they stick to their values? *Can* they stick to their values? Nearly all their traditional virtues – patience, tolerance, cool-headedness, wry humour, courtesy – are the product of richness and power. Isn't there a real danger that with riches and power these virtues will disappear?

A. Yes, there is a very real danger.

Q. Then why don't they panic?

A. They do, but very, very quietly.

Q. Are Trade Unions a real danger?

A. You bet.

Q. And what do the British do about it?

A. There were periods in British history – indeed in the history of all nations – when one or another layer of society, or group, or individual, grew much too strong. This could be the king, or parliament, or the barons, or the industrialists, or the feudal aristocracy, or the bankers, or the clergy. Their power had to be broken. In Britain it has always *been* broken. On one occasion a civil war was fought, on another occasion no civil war was fought. The problem of the Trade Unions will be solved, too. Probably without a civil war, which is a pity. A civil war would at least enliven the British scene.

Q. How would they fight a civil war?

A. Very, very quietly.

Q. Isn't there a danger of extremists gaining the upper hand?

A. Hard to tell. Probably not. The British, on the whole, are extreme moderates, passionate pacifists, rabid middle-of-the-roaders. But one cannot be sure.

Q. Isn't, then, a dictatorship or some other form of authoritarian regime a possibility?

A. Unlikely. The British are too used to solving their problems in committees, in open discussions. They are used to no-confidence motions, to letters to the editor, and just to opening their mouths and speaking up. Besides, they would laugh any would-be dictator off the face of Britain. When the Russians chased away the Czar, no democracy followed because they did not chase away Czarist *traditions*. Or take Uganda. We keep saying: 'You can't expect a Westminster-type democracy there, they don't have the tradition.' Similarly, we don't have the authoritarian tradition. Britain completely lacks practice in authoritarianism. They don't know how to be dictators; they don't know how to be slaves; they don't know how to be afraid of authority or the police.

Q. With all these splendid principles and lack of

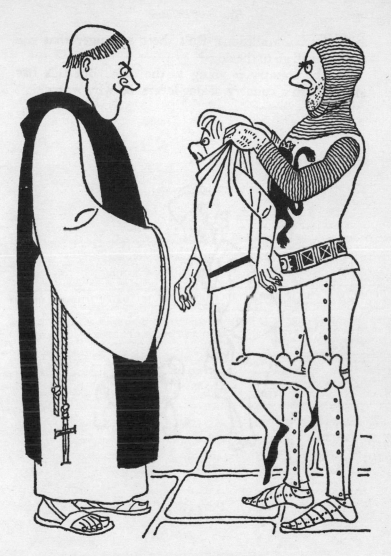

The power of the clergy

authoritarian traditions, isn't there a danger that the country will go to the dogs?

A. The country *is* going to the dogs. But this has always been a country of dog-lovers. So why worry?

ON FIDDLING THROUGH

You can be as rude about the English as you wish, they positively like it. In any case you cannot be as rude about them as they are about themselves. Years after the First World War – when I was a child in Hungary – people were still laughing about the war communiqués of the Austro-Hungarian High Command. Every rout they had suffered became an 'orderly and planned withdrawal'; giving up whole provinces and running away became 'straightening the lines', and chaos and final collapse was 'strategic reorganisation'. In World War II it took me three years in London to get used to the relish – the positive joy – with which the English reported their defeats, disasters and routs. The greater the disaster, the greater the joy. By the time I got used to the disasters – and started enjoying them myself – it was too late; they had started winning victories and went on to win the war.

It is *praising* the British that creates problems. Praising is 'patronising', 'slapping on the back', and that they find offensive. Tell them 'you are a great nation' and most of them will laugh because no one has spoken of 'great nations' in Europe since the death of de Gaulle. Others will not laugh but will feel offended: who the hell are

you to distribute medals? If you want to be polite, call
them a 'once great nation' – or better still: 'a once great
nation now in decline'. If you want to flatter them, call
them lazy, indolent, inefficient, inept and left behind
even by Luxemburg and Andorra. Bernard Shaw made a
fortune by calling the English stupid and repeating the
charge for six decades, because cleverness is a virtue they
particularly despise.

*   *   *

When I first came here, the British were obviously un-
prepared – both militarily and psychologically – for the
war which was about to break out. They shrugged their
shoulders and reassured jumpy aliens, like myself, that
'we shall muddle through'. *Muddling through* was one
of the most popular phrases for years; but I do not think
I have heard it even once since the outbreak of the
present economic crisis. The British, as I have said, are –
alas – getting cleverer. This is the Age of the Fiddle.
From middle-middle class downwards everybody must
have a fiddle. A fiddle helps; a fiddle solves all the
problems; a fiddle is the secret of success or at least of
survival. Instead of muddling through, nowadays we
are fiddling through. If you come here from abroad,
bring your own fiddle and you may get on top. The top
cheat – the Fiddler on the Roof – is the hero of the hour.

THE GENERATION GAP

'GREAT craftsmen? Their days are over,' said Mr S.,
that genius of a patisserie maker, one of the great craftsmen left in this country for whom money is nothing,
quality and satisfaction of the customer is everything.

I am no sweet-eater. Old aunts hated me as a child
because I never touched the cakes they had made for me
with so much care and love. I still would not touch anybody else's chocolate cakes with a barge-pole. But Mr S.
is in a class of his own. Perhaps you are not fond of
Harold Pinter or Tom Stoppard – excellent playwrights
though they are – but still raise your hat to Shakespeare;
you may not be impressed by Brasilia, yet you are awe-
struck by Venice; you may not be fond of pop music but
you are haunted by the Ninth Symphony. In other
words, Mr S. is the Shakespeare-cum-Beethoven of the
Chelsea Bun.

'When I retire or die,' he went on ruefully, 'that will
be the end of my craft. Nobody will produce this sort
of stuff; and if someone produced it people wouldn't
appreciate it. They would buy and enjoy frozen muck at
the supermarket. Young people are no good. I have
nobody, just nobody, to pass my business and skill on to.'

'I thought you had a son,' I interjected.

Mr S. got angry.

'Yes, I do have a son. He's a good-for-nothing. A dead loss.'

I couldn't ask *which* prison he was in, so I put it more tactfully: 'What is he doing?'

He sighed deeply: 'He's a professor of mathematics at London University.'

IS THE ECONOMY
REALLY ON THE MEND?

WHEN I was young, I heard this joke in Budapest. A man goes to the rabbi and complains: 'Rabbi, I am in despair. At my wits' end. Life is unbearable. We just cannot stand it any longer. There are nine of us – my wife and myself, her parents and five children – and we all live in one room. What can I do?'

The rabbi tells him kindly: 'Take the goat in.'

The man is incredulous: 'In the *room*?'

'Yes, in the room. Do as you are told. Take the goat in and come back in a week's time.'

A week later the man comes back, half dead: 'Rabbi, we just cannot stand it. All of us are going crazy. The goat is filthy. Loud. Dirty. It stinks. It makes a mess.'

The rabbi told him: 'Go home and let the goat out. And come back in a week's time.'

A radiantly happy man visits the rabbi a week later.

'Life is beautiful, rabbi. Lovely. We all enjoy every minute of life. No goat: only the nine of us.'

The same has happened to the British economy. The bank rate – or minimum lending rate – went up to fifteen per cent. Then down to twelve and a half. Now the

'Rabbi, I am in despair –'

country is rapturously happy and oozing optimism. How wonderful: a lending-rate as low as twelve and a half per cent.

All that has happened is that the goat has been taken out of the British economy.

HOW TO LOSE AN EMPIRE

To lose an Empire is a bit of a shock. I personally did not like it at all. I am that mildly left-wing liberal who has always preached that we (it became 'we' for me after the war) ought to give it up. But I never expected that Attlee would follow my advice. It is very satisfactory to advocate a noble deed; but it is quite shocking to see responsible people acting on your advice.

The change of atmosphere came very suddenly to the whole world. Before the war Hitler declared that the Sudetenland was his last territorial demand in Europe and all he wanted was the return of the former German colonies. I do not remember one single voice – including African or Asian voices – declaring that the Age of Colonies was over, that all nations and tribes wished to be independent now and that the idea of imperialism was, or should be, dead. People said instead that it was quite reasonable on Herr Hitler's part, we would see what we could do. We hinted that Hitler could have other people's colonies – that would be only fair – but not ours. There were some whispers about the Germans having been harsh and cruel colonisers, not so decent and universally beloved as the British, the French, the Dutch, the Belgians or the Portuguese. But, I repeat, not one single voice told Hitler: 'Colonies? No, you cannot have colonies. As a matter of fact, *no one* can have colonies any more.'

The change on this matter was as thorough as that in people's attitude to female nakedness. But at least between the times when a Victorian lady could not be persuaded to show her ankles and the times when a neo-Elizabethan lady could not be persuaded to cover up her breasts, a whole century passed. But it took only a few short years for nations to cover up their colonies with a blush, hide their dominions, apologise humbly for their former mistake of running a disorderly Empire and living on the earnings of its natives. So-called freedom and independence was granted to all and sundry whether they wanted it or not.

No doubt it is the speed with which it happened that has made losing an Empire a bit of a shock. It is like an individual losing a limb. You can't help getting used to your left foot and you do miss it when you have to part with it. But people react to such a disaster in diverse ways. Some people become bitter and full of hatred and blame others, starting with God, for their misfortune. Others, who have lost a hand, are determined to show that they can become virtuoso piano-players (like Ravel's famous friend) or become football players without legs (like a young and admirably brave little boy I know). Others despair and come to the conclusion that life is not worth living any more. Others look at their tragedy wisely and realise that the dreadful loss is also – like all losses – a gain: you can discover certain aspects, beauties and values in life which would have remained undiscovered but for your misfortune. If you are wise enough

'How dare you, sir!'

you will accept your limitations and turn to new fields in search of new satisfactions. A legless man may be wiser, more intelligent, better educated, more widely read, a better chess player and a more knowledgeable stamp-collector than a man with two legs; but he will not be able to run faster.

If you want to become a modern Englishman you must make up your mind which of the main groups you wish to join.

1. *The Colditz Group.* This group holds that Empire or no Empire, we are still top nation. We licked those bloody Nazis single handed (except that we did not). Never mind that the pound is slipping, it is Colditz that counts. The German economy may be powerful and we may be beggars or at least borrowers (what's the difference?) but so what? During the war (which ended over thirty years ago, about the length of time that passed between Napoleon and the Crimean War, another era in history), well, during the war the brilliant British outwitted those dull Germans. The Germans were brutal, coarse, cruel and dimwitted; the British noble, heroic, indomitable, and gallant. If you doubt this, read any trashy novel or watch even trashier films on television. You can see two a day. It was our finest hour. We – the Colditz Group – want to live that finest hour forever. Yes we want to escape from something – as everybody in Colditz was always escaping.

2. *The Palmerston Group.* Or you may maintain – as millions do – that absolutely nothing has, in fact, changed. Queen Victoria is still on the throne, Lord Palmerston is still our Foreign Secretary. Recalcitrant tribal chiefs will be birched and – in the case of grave

unrest – gunboats dispatched. Some members of this group may have noticed that we do not have India any more; but we still have Gibraltar, Hong Kong and the Falkland Islands. World-wide responsibilities.

Palmerstonians look down with a superior but condescendingly benevolent smile on all other nations. Foreigners are still funny. The Germans have a silly language, whoever heard of putting the predicate always at the end of the sentence? The Americans are even more laughable – they speak English with an American accent, not in our distinguished Cockney or Geordie. The Chinese are Chinks, the Japanese Japs, the Germans are Krauts.

All is well, really the main problem is to keep poor, sick Albert alive because our good Queen Victoria would be very upset if he died.

Only the British are real people, who can be respected, with a few exceptions who are no good at all:
a) the working classes;
b) the lower-middle-classes;
c) business-people, executives and all people in trade;
d) black people;
e) brown people;
f) Jews;
g) foreigners;
h) Londoners and other city-dwellers (if you live in the country); and
i) country bumpkins (if you live in London or another city).

But as all these amount to only 187 per cent of the population, you can justly be proud of your people.

A member of this group once remarked: 'Running a

vast Empire does – inevitably – create arrogance. The Empire is gone; let's stick to the arrogance. We must keep *something*.'

3. *The Staunch Independents.* Very well, say members of this group, we accept reality. But we do not give up our national pride. Running to the International Monetary Fund or the EEC and others for money is undignified. But we accept no conditions. We shall never – never! – allow foreigners to run our economy. They might cure it. Look what these Germans, Swiss, Swedes etc did to their own economy.

4. *The Little Englander.* England is gone. It has become a country of no importance. It is an off-shore island. A new Jamaica. We know it was wrong to rule two-thirds of the world. Our mistake. We do apologise. We'll never do it again. True, we still have some virtues and assets. We still have some brilliant writers, a magnificent political sense, great courage, tremendous experience, unrivalled skills in some fields but all this is really not our fault. We have not been able to get rid of these virtues quickly enough to fit our new, modest position in the world, but we shall do our best. We shall try to sink lower, difficult though it is, with all our gifts. But we'll try. We won't give up. Sorry for being alive.

5. *The Mikes Group.* Or you can join me. This is what this whole book is about. We will say – and we may be right, or we may be too pessimistic – that nations grow old, just like individuals. They lose their competitive spirit; their ambitions; their virility. In other words, they grow up, become wise, likeable and humane.

If you have to become poor, learn to enjoy your poverty but do not become a showing-off, conceited *nouveau pauvre*; if you become weak, find new strength in your weakness; if you have to decay, decay with elegance and grace. An ageing gentleman cannot be a great tennis champion, a devastating fast bowler or a record-breaking long-distance runner; on the other hand those loud-mouthed, vulgar youths cannot be shrewd, mature and wise old men.

HOW TO BECOME A COLONY

THE British are brave people. They can face anything, except reality. You can tell them that they have lost an Empire and that they are slowly sliding out of the first eleven of countries: that is obvious. But you cannot tell them – so don't – that they are being colonised themselves.

They are being colonised by rival powers. First of all, they seem to have become a colony of Saudi Arabia. Sometimes, looking at certain districts of London, you would think that there can be no more Arabs left in Riyadh. There must be more sheiks in the London casinos than in all of Jeddah. During the hot, long summer of 1976 the country was actually being turned into a desert, with a few oases here and there. We have even got the oil – as befits a country which other countries want to colonise.

The Arab menace, however, is much less serious than it seems. It is true that they buy up half of the country; it is true that they fill the most expensive British nursing homes with patients grand or humble, to such an extent, that in these establishments all notices, menus etc. are printed in Arabic with an English translation (for the staff). But the Arabs, at least, return to Britain a substantial part of the money they make on their oil. Not so much through the nursing homes – although what they rake in is not inconsiderable – as through the gaming tables. This is fair and decent of them. Whenever they raise the price of their oil by ten per cent, they also raise their losses on roulette and *chemin de fer* by the same amount.

The Indians, too, are getting even with the British. Small trade – as a first step – is being taken over by Indians and Pakistanis. In Fulham, where I live, one shop after another has passed into Indian hands: the newsagent's, the grocer's, the greengrocer's, the small post office, the chemist and so on. I am not sure that the Indians were so pleased when we took over their land but I, personally, am delighted by their turning Fulham into an Indian colony, with my television-repairer as its viceroy.

The small, dingy English grocer-shop has become a splendid little supermarket; at the post-office service – and courtesy – have improved beyond recognition; the newsagents – unlike their English predecessors – send me the papers *I have ordered* and they arrive early in the morning. And the Indians keep their shops open at all the hours when you want to shop, not only at the so-called regular hours when you do not or cannot. The new Indian Empire is heartily welcome, by me at least, but alas there are limits to its expansion. At Earl's Court – particularly around Gloucester Road – the Indian Empire reaches Arab territory and this Empire is more staunchly defended than ever our Empire was. No question of granting independence to Gloucester Road.

Even the EEC countries are quick to seize their

Regular hours

chances. I wrote some years ago that the Common Market ought to beware because Britain is not, in fact, joining Europe but is founding a new Empire. I could not have been more wrong. It is our EEC partners who are colonising us. Britain is being invaded. The Ministry of Defence keeps a sinister silence about this new invasion which is much more effective than William's amateurish attempt was in 1066.

Anyone who has eyes, can see what is happening. A large foreign army, broken up into small units, is arriving day after day at Dover and Harwich. They are armed with travellers cheques and foreign currencies with great power of penetration. They bring with them vast shopping bags disguised as motor-cars and shooting brakes. The groups look quite innocent, except that from time to time their eyes roll ferociously and they utter a menacing battle-cry which sounds like: 'Marks and Spencer! Marks and Spencer!'

There is one great difference between the new invasion and that of William: William's army has stayed in England for a thousand years and there is little hope that their descendants will ever leave. The new invaders grab their loot and withdraw almost immediately.

Once upon a time it was the British who invaded strange lands and got hold of foreign treasure in exchange for beads and other worthless bric-à-brac. Now its our turn to be invaded, and the invaders pay with something called pound sterling which they can pick up on their shores for practically nothing. No doubt the moral is: 'Plus ça change. ...'

ON CEASING TO BE AN ISLAND

I COULD put up with all this. What I cannot bear is our giving up our most sacred heritage. Look what's happening.

I have spent the best years of my life becoming a true Englishman and now the whole country is turning alien, lock, stock and barrel. Britain joining Europe was as if the Pope had turned Anglican or Ghadafi had emigrated to Israel and joined a kibbutz. And even that was not all. Decimal currency has come to stay. Where are the glorious days when every wretched foreign visitor was puzzled, foxed and driven to despair when he had to calculate what he'd have left from seven and six after paying six and eleven? Where are the glorious days of the halfcrown – the half of a non-existent crown? Why is the guinea dead? What is happening to Fahrenheit – that completely senseless measurement of temperature, invented by an East Prussian but so supremely English? As a system, it was rotten, of course, but that's not the point. No bloody foreigner could understand it – not even Herr Fahrenheit, I am sure – and that was the glory of it.

I do not mind Britain becoming decadent but I very much mind Britain ceasing to be an island. And that's what's happening. Not because of the aeroplane; not because of the speed of communications; not because of the invention of nuclear power; not even because of our being colonised by Arabs, Indians and Europeans. The crunch has come with invasion by the decimal point – by kilos, grams, and millimetres, by a logical, easy system of measurement. This is our final humiliation.

I hate being a prophet of doom but I must speak up. When the furlong, the chain, the rod, pole and perch, the peck, the bushel and the gill are gone, Britain as an island will have disappeared and the country will have become a suburb of Brussels.

ENVOI

LET us not get hysterical. What does it matter whether we are colonising the Punjab or the Punjab is colonising Fulham? . . . But, you may ask, if that does not matter, what does?

The virtues the English still possess matter. The tolerance, the courtesy, the still fairly decent table manners, the sly good humour, the passion for queueing, the self-deprecation and dislike of flattery, the cool-headedness (even the cold-bloodedness – there's something to be said for not making too much of sex), the gift for double-think which makes it possible to foist airfields and motorways onto other people's doorsteps and refuse to have them on your own. . . . All these virtues, being the result of power and affluence, are as I have said disappearing. But they are disappearing very slowly – slowly enough for me. I am disappearing slowly myself.

Many people are leaving this country: too many strikes, too little public transport, the falling pound and standard of living, the sinking economy, the uncertainty of their children's future: they want no more of all this. Good luck to them.

I, on the other hand, am going to stay even if Britain becomes a desert island with me as her Robinson Crusoe.

Our sly good humour

That, when I come to think of it, would have considerable advantages. The pound sterling would cease to exist so it could fall no lower. If I were alone, Britain would at last be free of class distinctions – the only way, I am sure, that this could happen. Or is it? As a British subject I could always look down on myself as a former bloody foreigner, and as a former middle-class intellectual I could despise the agricultural labourer I would have to become. Even one man can keep up class-warfare if he's really determined.

Even with other people around I like it here. Not always and not everything. But on the whole I like it here very much. Besides, this country accepted me in my hour of need and I am not abandoning her in *her* hour of need (although I have a vague suspicion that I am of not too much help). I have changed my country once and this is, I feel, enough for any man for a lifetime. Let England and me decay together. We are both decaying in good company.

Let me say one more thing in conclusion. When I wrote that other little book, thirty years ago, I admired the English enormously but did not like them very much; today I admire them much less but love them much more.

A LETTER FROM ANDRÉ DEUTSCH

My dear George,

Dear George,

We have been good friends for a very long time. We really met properly here in England, that last summer before the Second World War: when I arrived from Hungary you were already a settled citizen of London. We had known each other in Budapest, of course – but at that time I was still a little boy and you were a grown-up young journalist going out with beautiful actresses, much too sophisticated to talk to your younger brother or to me.

That age-gap closed, but it was not until the summer of 1945 that you did your first good deed for me. I can tell you what you were doing on the Isle of Wight – you and your wife were on holiday there. You rang me and said 'I have written something. Come for the week-end and read it.' So I drove down in my battered little Hillman Minx, and there was the manuscript which became *How to be an Alien*.

I read it at a sitting and naturally loved it, but said that you must write a little more. We agreed that, as you were not well-known in England, we would have to find you an illustrator who was famous as well as good. We drew up a list of names, and at its top was the name of a man I have never met, Nicolas Bentley. So it was through you that I met Nick, who became a great friend and my partner – something else to thank you for.

We have published books together now, and it has been great fun, in spite of our many arguments. I have always suspected that there is a little Paul Getty inside you wanting to get out, and I know that the person wanting to get

out of me is a clown. You and Paul Getty, me and Grock –
it sounds an ill-assorted team, but I think that we haven't
done too badly.

It gives me enormous pleasure to make this one volume
of your three famous books about the British. If I am not
an inimitable and decadent alien it is not for want of
studying the texts, but because I drew out of them their
inner meaning as revealed through your present title, and
thanks to you, dear friend, have become a true Brit.*

Yours ever

André.

* As you can tell the way I said above 'we haven't done
too badly' instead of 'we have been hugely successful'.

PENGUIN ONLINE

READ MORE IN PENGUIN

In every corner of the world, on every subject under the sun, Penguin represents quality and variety – the very best in publishing today.

For complete information about books available from Penguin – including Puffins, Penguin Classics and Arkana – and how to order them, write to us at the appropriate address below. Please note that for copyright reasons the selection of books varies from country to country.

In the United Kingdom: Please write to *Dept. EP, Penguin Books Ltd, Bath Road, Harmondsworth, West Drayton, Middlesex UB7 ODA*

In the United States: Please write to *Consumer Sales, Penguin Putnam Inc., P.O. Box 12289 Dept. B, Newark, New Jersey 07101-5289.* VISA and MasterCard holders call 1-800-788-6262 to order Penguin titles

In Canada: Please write to *Penguin Books Canada Ltd, 10 Alcorn Avenue, Suite 300, Toronto, Ontario M4V 3B2*

In Australia: Please write to *Penguin Books Australia Ltd, P.O. Box 257, Ringwood, Victoria 3134*

In New Zealand: Please write to *Penguin Books (NZ) Ltd, Private Bag 102902, North Shore Mail Centre, Auckland 10*

In India: Please write to *Penguin Books India Pvt Ltd, 11 Community Centre, Panchsheel Park, New Delhi 110017*

In the Netherlands: Please write to *Penguin Books Netherlands bv, Postbus 3507, NL-1001 AH Amsterdam*

In Germany: Please write to *Penguin Books Deutschland GmbH, Metzlerstrasse 26, 60594 Frankfurt am Main*

In Spain: Please write to *Penguin Books S. A., Bravo Murillo 19, 1° B, 28015 Madrid*

In Italy: Please write to *Penguin Italia s.r.l., Via Benedetto Croce 2, 20094 Corsico, Milano*

In France: Please write to *Penguin France, Le Carré Wilson, 62 rue Benjamin Baillaud, 31500 Toulouse*

In Japan: Please write to *Penguin Books Japan Ltd, Kaneko Building, 2-3-25 Koraku, Bunkyo-Ku, Tokyo 112*

In South Africa: Please write to *Penguin Books South Africa (Pty) Ltd, Private Bag X14, Parkview, 2122 Johannesburg*

READ MORE IN PENGUIN

HUMOUR

Scorn with Extra Bile   Matthew Parris

'A bucketful of invective, ridicule and curses' *Sunday Times*. 'Political correctness is flouted on every page . . . It is in the puncturing of pomp and hypocrisy that the real gems are to be found' *The Times*

Lady Chatterley's Lover according to Spike Milligan

In Spike Milligan's intense, steaming, palpitating, lustful, unexpurgated retelling of Lady Chatterley's romps with a member of the lower orders (with footnotes), many hitherto unknown aspects are revealed (as well as – all too frequently the gamekeeper's delicate white loins).

Harry Enfield and his Humorous Chums   Harry Enfield

'Here, for the first time, are all my Chums in one splendid package. Plus, how they came about, the ones that got away, the ones I love best, the ones I hate. Read this book, admire, worship and revere me.'

The Desperate Woman's Guide to Diet and Exercise   Jo Nesbitt

Are you getting too serious about counting calories and working off that extra layer of flab? Try the best antidote of all and see the funny side of it – a sure way of keeping a level head when everything else is turning pear-shaped!

The Log   Craig Charles

Craig says: 'I've often thought: what would it be like to be the last human in the Universe? What in Space would I do?' Write something for posterity, perhaps? An attempt to chronicle the human race during its entire turbulent history? In other words, *A Dwarfer's Guide to Everything*.

Philosophy Football   Mark Perryman

The amazing tale of a make-believe team, *Philosophy Football* is the story of what might have happened to the world's greatest thinkers if their brains had been in their boots instead of their heads . . .